THE GREAT BRITISH BAKE OFF

CHRISTMAS

LIZZIE KAMENETZKY
WITH RECIPES FROM
BAKE OFF JUDGES & CONTESTANTS

BBC
BOOKS

3 5 7 9 10 8 6 4 2

BBC Books, an imprint of Ebury Publishing
20 Vauxhall Bridge Road,
London, SW1V 2SA

BBC Books is part of the Penguin Random House group of companies
whose address can be found at: global.penguinrandomhouse.com

Penguin
Random House
UK

First published in 2014 by BBC Books, an imprint of Ebury Publishing.

www.eburypublishing.co.uk

A CIP catalogue record for this book is available from the British Library

ISBN 978 1 849 90696 8

Executive Producer: Anna Beattie
BBC Commissioning Executive: Emma Willis
Editorial Director: Lizzy Gray
Project Editor: Kate Fox
Design: Allies Design
Typesetting and layout: Jim Smith
Photography: Laura Edwards
Food Stylist: Lizzie Kamenetzky
Prop Stylist: Polly Webb-Wilson
Production: Helen Everson and Rebecca Jones

Printed and bound by Mohn Media Mohndruck GmbH in Germany

Penguin Random House is committed to a sustainable future for our business, our readers
and our planet. This book is made from Forest Stewardship Council® certified paper.

CONTENTS

INTRODUCTION

Christmas is an undisputed highlight of the winter calendar. As the nights draw in and the days shorten, thoughts turn to planning our festive celebrations.

There is something about this time of year that draws you into the warmth and glow of the kitchen. Baking is an inherent part of the festivities and the familiar scents of cinnamon, cloves, ginger and nutmeg wafting round our homes are as much a part of the Christmas season as the giving of gifts and lighting of candles.

For most of us, Christmas is steeped in tradition and annual rituals. Yet for a festival that has its roots in medieval times, its common celebrations actually developed fairly recently. Queen Victoria and Prince Albert popularised many of the traditions we observe today. Cards, crackers, decorated trees and the giving of elaborate gifts all emerged over the course of the 19th century thanks to the pair's fond enthusiasm for Christmas, and much of the dinner we consider 'traditional' took shape during their reign. Wealthy Victorian families started to reject beef and goose as the centrepiece of the meal in favour of fatted turkeys; while the Victorian love of all things sweet also saw the mince pie's meat filling replaced by today's fruity offering. Christmas has the ability to transport you back to your own childhood, to another time: if for you the season is all about getting your loved ones together for a generous dose of merriment, eating and drinking, you'll find you haven't strayed far from the quintessential family Christmas captured by Charles Dickens in his much-loved story, 'A Christmas Carol'.

This book will accompany you through your festive season. Starting in Advent and the first few days of December, there are recipes to help you through every stage of the countdown to the big day and run-up to New Year's Eve, as well as the events themselves. There are timeless classics for those who stand by tradition, but if you're looking to shake things up a bit this year or want a new challenge, there are inspired ideas for putting something a little bit different on your Christmas table.

Thinking ahead is one of the most important things to keep you sane over this period, so there are plenty of dishes and bakes to make in advance or freeze so that you don't get caught short. And even if no one quite finishes the turkey, ham or Christmas pudding, there are lifesaving ideas for reinventing your leftovers. To round the year off, the chapter on New Year's Eve is filled with recipes for party canapés, indulgent meals for a smaller gathering and showstopping desserts to enjoy as the clock strikes 12.

This book is the ultimate guide to Christmas baking, however you celebrate the season. Merry Christmas to you all.

THE COUNTDOWN BEGINS

THE COUNTDOWN BEGINS

December is the perfect time to start baking and thinking about the festive preparations ahead.

'Stir up Sunday', which falls on the last Sunday before Advent, was historically the day to make your Christmas puddings, cake and mincemeat for mince pies. Making them this far in advance allows the flavours to deepen and develop to become rich, dark and fragrant. It is traditional to get the whole family involved with the pudding, each stirring the bowl clockwise for luck.

Once the holidays begin, kids can get involved in the Christmas bakes, too. Advent Calendar Biscuits (page 17) make a wonderful edible alternative to the more commercial, image-led advent calendars. Fill the house with the scent of dough and spices as you bake a Gingerbread Nativity (page 21), or Panforte (page 27), one of Italy's oldest sweets dating back to the 13th century.

To decorate the house, evergreen wreaths have symbolized life since pagan times. We hang them during the Christmas season, the darkest period of the year, to remind us that Spring will come. The sticky Cinnamon and Raspberry Whirl Wreath on page 18 is a delicious homage to this ancient tradition.

Not everything is about Christmas, however, and as the big day draws near, a few quick and simple bakes for busy days are essential. If you always have some puff pastry on standby, you can turn it into a tasty tart, such as the Beetroot, Watercress and Goats' Cheese Tart on page 31, in a matter of moments – just perfect for this hectic time of year.

ADVENT CALENDAR BISCUITS

This year, try something different from the traditional or chocolate advent calendar:
this will look so impressive sitting on your mantlepiece or even strung from a branch.

MAKES 30–32

YOU WILL NEED: NUMBER-SHAPED AND CHRISTMAS-SHAPED PASTRY CUTTERS

115g unsalted butter, softened
115g caster sugar
1 teaspoon vanilla extract
1 small egg

225g plain flour
¾ teaspoon baking powder
a good pinch of salt

To decorate
rollable fondant icing OR icing
sugar and coloured food dyes

1 Cream the butter, sugar and vanilla with a hand-held electric whisk until light and fluffy. Add the egg and whisk until combined.

2 In a separate bowl, combine the flour, baking powder and salt. Slowly add the flour mixture to the butter mixture, mixing until completely combined but not dry and crumbly; you may not need all the flour mixture.

3 Bring the dough together with your hands and shape into a disc. Working very quickly, as your dough is soft, roll it out between 2 large sheets of baking paper to about 5–6mm thick. Place the rolled dough in its paper on a baking sheet, and chill for 30 minutes. Meanwhile, heat the oven to 180°C/350°F/gas 4.

4 Remove the chilled dough from the fridge and use different shaped cutters, about 6cm, to cut out 30–32 biscuits from the dough. You can use number cutters to cut out the numbers 1–24 in some of your biscuits or you can ice the numbers later when decorating. Arrange the cut biscuits on 2 lightly greased baking sheets, making sure they aren't touching, place in the heated oven and bake for 10–12 minutes until golden. Whilst still warm, use the end of a

piping nozzle or a skewer to make a hole in each biscuit (for threading the string). Leave to cool for 10 minutes on the baking sheets, then transfer to a wire rack to cool completely.

5 To decorate, cut out rollable fondant icing into shapes to match the shapes of the biscuits. Brush with a little water and stick each to its corresponding biscuit, remaking the hole for the ribbon in the icing. Alternatively, make up coloured icings by mixing icing sugar with a little water and the colour of your choice, to make a smooth pipeable paste, then spoon into small piping bags fitted with small plain piping nozzles and pipe onto the biscuits. If you haven't used number cutters, now pipe the numbers 1–24 on 24 on your biscuits and decorate the rest however you like. When dry, thread the biscuits with string or ribbons of different lengths and hang from a tree branch, or pin to a board or mantlepiece.

THINKING AHEAD

This sugar biscuit dough freezes really well, so make up a double batch (using a large rather than small egg) and freeze half to use later.

CINNAMON AND RASPBERRY WHIRL WREATH

This delicious wreath is made from a sweet, enriched dough coated in fruity jam.
It emerges from the oven with the aroma of freshly baked bread and yuletide spirit.
Once cool, adorn your wreath with a festive ribbon and eat within 3 days.

MAKES 1 LARGE WREATH

350ml full-fat milk

60g caster sugar

10 cardamom pods, crushed

85g unsalted butter

1 x 7g sachet fast-action
   dried yeast

1 medium egg

500g plain flour, plus extra
   for dusting

1 teaspoon salt

For the filling

4 tablespoons raspberry jam

2 teaspoons ground cinnamon
   mixed with 2 teaspoons
   caster sugar

1 Warm the milk in a pan with the sugar and cardamom. Once steaming, add the butter and let it melt, then remove from the heat and leave to infuse for 4-5 minutes. Pour through a sieve into a jug, cool until only just warm, then add the yeast and egg and mix well.

2 Sift the flour into a large bowl with the salt and make a well in the centre. Add the liquid and mix with your hands until it all comes together. If it is a little too dry add a splash more milk, and if it feels a little too wet you can add a little more flour, but err on the wetter side to avoid a dry dough.

3 Turn out onto a lightly floured work surface and knead for 5-10 minutes until smooth and elastic. Return to the clean bowl, cover with a clean tea towel and leave in a warm place for about 1 hour or until doubled in size.

4 Punch down the dough with your knuckles and turn out onto a lightly floured surface. Roll it out to a rectangle about 25 x 45cm, with the long side towards you. Spread the jam evenly over the dough and sprinkle with the cinnamon mixture, leaving a 2cm border on the long side closest to you.

5 Roll the dough up as tightly as you can, starting from the long side furthest from you. Slice the dough in half along its length to expose the layers. Starting at one end, cross the pieces over each other, keeping the exposed layers uppermost, working down the length of the dough, then transfer to a lined baking sheet and shape into a wreath by folding the four ends over each other to continue the plait.

CONTINUED

6 Cover with a clean tea towel or lightly greased clingfilm and leave in a warm place for 1 hour, or until doubled in size. Meanwhile, heat the oven to 180°C/350°F/gas 4.

7 Place the wreath in the heated oven and bake for 30–35 minutes until lightly golden, then remove from the oven and transfer to a wire rack to cool before serving.

TIP

If your kitchen is a little cold, heat your oven to 50°C/120°F/lowest gas setting, then turn it off. Place the bowl of dough in the warm, but switched off, oven to prove.

THINKING AHEAD

Freeze the proved, unbaked wreath on a baking sheet until solid, then wrap well in baking paper and foil or clingfilm and freeze for up to 3 months. Defrost fully before baking.

GINGERBREAD NATIVITY

Gingerbread is traditionally used to make houses as it is the perfect dough to build with: strong and tough, and able to withstand slight weight without crumbling. Unless your freeform cutting is very good, or you want to use hand-drawn templates, you can buy nativity cutters online. Pictured overleaf.

YOU WILL NEED: NATIVITY PASTRY CUTTERS OR TEMPLATES; A SMALL PIPING BAG FITTED WITH A VERY SMALL, PLAIN NOZZLE

125g unsalted butter
100g light muscovado sugar
3 tablespoons golden syrup
300g plain flour
1 scant teaspoon bicarbonate of soda

1½ tablespoons ground ginger
rollable white fondant icing
200g icing sugar, plus extra for dusting
silver dragées

1 Melt the butter with the sugar and syrup in a pan. Mix the flour, bicarbonate of soda and ground ginger in a large bowl. Pour in the butter mixture and stir to make a stiff dough. Roll out on a sheet of baking paper to 3mm thick and chill for 10–15 minutes. Meanwhile, heat the oven to 190°C/375°F/gas 5.

2 Use nativity cutters to cut out shapes for the stable and figures from the chilled dough, then re-roll the trimmings and cut out the largest rectangle you can, for the base. Place the shapes and base on 2 baking sheets lined with non-stick or silicon paper, transfer to the heated oven and bake for 12 minutes.

3 Remove from the oven and, whilst still hot, trim any edges of your stable so they are nice and straight; this will make them easier to stick together later. Allow to cool on the sheets for 10 minutes before transferring to a wire rack to cool completely. You can then use a fine grater to smooth and even out the biscuits to get a really straight edge for sticking.

4 To decorate, you can ice your biscuits in a number of ways. If you want solid icing, roll out ready-made fondant on a surface lightly dusted with icing sugar. Cut out shapes using your nativity cutter. Brush the corresponding biscuit with a little water then stick the icing to it and set aside to dry.

5 Mix the icing sugar with enough water to make a thick but pipeable icing. Spoon into a small piping bag fitted with a very small plain nozzle. Use either to attach dragées and decorations to your fondant-covered biscuits, or to pipe detail on the un-iced biscuits.

6 Arrange your nativity by sticking the pieces together with the piping icing (see Tip). Some straw or hay makes a lovely artistic addition to your scene.

TIP

Be patient when assembling your nativity. Make sure your icing is really lovely and thick and stick the stable together first, using matchboxes or cotton reels to support the positioned pieces and figures as they dry.

MARY'S CLASSIC CHRISTMAS CAKE

MAKES 1 CAKE
YOU WILL NEED: A 23CM ROUND, DEEP CAKE TIN, GREASED AND LINED WITH
A DOUBLE LAYER OF GREASEPROOF PAPER; A 28CM ROUND CAKE BOARD

For the cake
175g raisins
350g glacé cherries, halved, rinsed, thoroughly dried and quartered
500g currants
350g sultanas
150ml brandy, plus extra for feeding the cake
finely grated zest of 2 oranges
250g butter, softened
250g light muscovado sugar

4 medium eggs
1 tablespoon black treacle
75g blanched almonds, chopped
75g self-raising flour
175g plain flour
1½ teaspoons ground mixed spice

To finish and decorate
about 3 tablespoons apricot jam, sieved and warmed

icing sugar, for dusting
675g almond paste
1 x quantity Royal Icing (see below)

For the royal icing
3 medium egg whites
675g icing sugar, sifted
3 teaspoons lemon juice
1½ teaspoons glycerine

1 Put all the dried fruit in a container, pour over the brandy and stir in the orange zest. Cover with a lid and leave to soak for 3 days, stirring daily.

2 Heat the oven to 140°C/275°F/gas 1. Put the butter, sugar, eggs, treacle and almonds in a very large bowl and beat well. Add the flours and mixed spice and mix thoroughly until blended. Stir in the soaked fruit, spoon into the prepared cake tin and level the surface.

3 Place in the centre of the heated oven and bake for about 4–4½ hours or until the cake feels firm to the touch and is a rich golden brown. Check after 2 hours and, if the cake is a perfect colour, cover with foil. When cooked, a skewer inserted into the centre should come out clean. Leave to cool in the tin.

4 When cool, pierce the cake at intervals with a fine skewer and feed with a little extra brandy. Wrap the completely cold cake in a double layer of greaseproof paper and again in foil and store in a cool place for up to 3 months, feeding at intervals with more brandy.

5 To decorate, stand the cake upside down, flat side uppermost, on the cake board. Brush the sides and the top of the cake with the warm apricot jam. Liberally dust the work surface with icing sugar and roll out the almond paste to a circle about 5cm larger all round than the surface of the cake. Keep moving the almond paste as you roll, checking that it is not sticking to the work surface, dusting the work surface with more icing sugar as necessary.

CONTINUED

6 Carefully lift the almond paste over the cake, using a rolling pin. Gently level and smooth the top of the paste with the rolling pin, then ease it down the sides of the cake, smoothing it at the same time. If necessary, neatly trim any excess almond paste from the base, using a small, sharp knife. Cover the cake loosely with baking parchment and leave for a few days to dry out before icing.

7 To make the royal icing, whisk the egg whites in a large bowl until frothy. Mix in the sifted icing sugar, a tablespoonful at a time. You can do this with a hand-held electric whisk, but keep the speed low. Stir in the lemon juice and glycerine and beat until very stiff and white, and it stands up in peaks.

8 Spread the icing evenly over the top and sides of the cake, using a palette knife. For a snow-peak effect, use a smaller palette knife to rough up the icing.

9 Loosely cover and leave overnight for the icing to harden a little, then wrap or store in an airtight container in a cool place until needed. Tie a festive ribbon round the middle and decorate the top with little Christmas decorations before serving.

TIP

Instead of covering with almond paste and royal icing, you could simply brush sieved warmed apricot jam over the top of the cooled cake, and then arrange glacé fruits and nuts over the jam. Brush again with jam.

THINKING AHEAD

You need to start making the cake 3 days in advance, and to allow the fruit to soak. The wrapped, un-iced cake will keep for up to 3 months, and will even improve over that time if you keep feeding it with brandy.

PANFORTE

This is a traditional Italian sweet to enjoy with coffee after a meal, and makes a great treat, packed full of spices, fruit and nuts. You can buy rice paper online and in some major supermarkets, but if you can't find it, simply line the tin with non-stick baking paper and peel away before serving.

SERVES 10–12

YOU WILL NEED: AN 18CM ROUND, LOOSE-BOTTOMED CAKE TIN, LINED WITH RICE PAPER

200g dried figs, finely chopped
100g dried apricots, finely chopped
75g honey
125g light muscovado sugar
1 teaspoon ground cinnamon
seeds of 12 cardamom pods, ground in a pestle and mortar
½ teaspoon ground cloves
a good grating of fresh nutmeg
a good twist of black pepper
75g chopped mixed peel
50g blanched almonds
50g shelled hazelnuts
50g nibbed pistachios
3 tablespoons plain flour
icing sugar, for dusting

1 Heat the oven to 170°C/325°F/gas 3. Put the figs and apricots in a pan with the honey, sugar and all the spices and pepper. Add a tablespoon or two of water and cook gently for about 10 minutes, then tip into a bowl; the mixture should be soft and sticky.

2 Add the mixed peel and nuts and mix well, then stir in the flour. Spoon the mixture into the prepared tin, place in the heated oven and bake for 40–45 minutes. Allow to cool in the tin completely, then remove. Cut into slices and dust with icing sugar to serve.

TIP

If you are making these as gifts you can double the recipe and make 4 smaller rounds to give away. Use 10cm mini cake tins instead of the 18cm one.

THINKING AHEAD

This keeps really well for several weeks, wrapped in non-stick baking paper in an airtight tin.

BEETROOT, WATERCRESS AND GOATS' CHEESE TART

Puff pastry is always great to have on standby as you can turn it into a tasty tart in a matter of moments. Beetroot is a natural friend of aniseedy flavours such as star anise, dill or tarragon, which bring out the earthy sweetness of this root veg.

SERVES 4–6

1 tablespoon olive oil
2 banana shallots, finely sliced
4 medium beetroots (about 500g), peeled and coarsely grated
3 tablespoons white wine vinegar
2 star anise

a small knob of unsalted butter
375g block of all-butter puff pastry, thawed if frozen
plain flour, for dusting
1 medium egg, beaten with 1 tablespoon milk
150ml crème fraîche

2 tablespoons finely chopped fresh dill
150g medium-soft goats' cheese log, crumbled
a large handful of watercress, dressed with a squeeze of lemon juice and a drizzle of extra virgin olive oil
salt and black pepper

1 Heat the oven to 220°C/425°F/gas 7. Heat the oil in a pan and gently fry the shallot for 5 minutes, until softened. Add the beetroot, vinegar, star anise, butter and 3 tablespoons water. Cook over a low heat, stirring occasionally, for 5–10 minutes until all the liquid has evaporated.

2 Meanwhile, roll out the pastry on a lightly floured surface to a rectangle about 25 x 38cm. Place on a baking sheet and score a line about 2cm in from the edge all around the pastry. Brush all over with the egg glaze and score the line a second time.

3 Place the pastry in the heated oven and bake for 10–12 minutes until risen and lightly golden. Remove from the oven and press down the centre of the pastry with your hands.

4 Remove the star anise from the beetroot and discard. Stir through the crème fraîche and dill, then season well with salt and pepper. Spread over the base of the tart and scatter the goats' cheese all over. Return the tart to the oven for 4–5 minutes until lovely and golden and the cheese has started to melt.

5 Remove from the oven and leave to cool for 10 minutes before scattering with watercress and serving.

TIP

Beetroots have a naughty habit of staining your hands so if you don't want to look like Lady Macbeth, wear rubber gloves whilst peeling and grating them!

MUSTARDY MAC 'N' CHEESE

Hearty and warming, mac 'n' cheese is perfect for long, dark winter days. Here, the rich, creamy, cheesy sauce is balanced by bacon and mustard, for a twist on the ultimate comfort food.

SERVES 8

YOU WILL NEED: A 2.75 LITRE OVENPROOF DISH, BUTTERED

1 litre full-fat milk

1 small onion, halved and
   studded with 3–4 cloves

2 fresh bay leaves

5 black peppercorns

2 teaspoons olive oil

200g streaky bacon, finely
   chopped

85g butter

75g plain flour

450g dried macaroni

350g grated hard cheeses,
   such as a mix of Cheddar
   and Gruyère

½ teaspoon cayenne pepper

1 teaspoon English mustard

1 tablespoon Dijon mustard

80ml double cream

50g fresh or dry breadcrumbs

3 tablespoons finely chopped
   flat-leaf parsley

salt and black pepper

1 Put the milk, clove-studded onion, bay leaves and peppercorns in a pan over a medium heat and bring to the boil. Remove from the heat and set aside for 10–15 minutes to infuse, then strain into a jug.

2 Heat the oil in a small frying pan and fry the bacon for 4–5 minutes until golden and crisp. Drain on kitchen paper and set aside.

3 Melt the butter in a pan, add the flour and cook gently, stirring, for about 30 seconds. Gradually stir in the milk over a low heat, a little at a time, until you have a thick, smooth sauce, then simmer very gently for 2–3 minutes.

4 Meanwhile, heat the oven to 200°C/400°F/ gas 6. Cook the macaroni in a large pan of boiling salted water for 10 minutes, or until just tender. Drain and return to the pan.

5 Stir all but a handful of the cheese into the sauce, then add the cayenne, mustards and cream. Season with salt and pepper and stir the sauce into the cooked macaroni with the crispy bacon. Pour into the buttered ovenproof dish. Mix the breadcrumbs with the remaining cheese and the parsley. Sprinkle over the macaroni, place in the heated oven and bake for 15–20 minutes until gorgeously golden and bubbling. Leave to stand for 5 minutes before serving.

CREAMY PORK, APPLE AND LEEK OPEN PIE

Pies are wonderful things, but so many of them are time-consuming labours of love, best made when you have a bit of a window to prepare the filling in advance or stock the freezer. This one is a cheat's pie, ready in time for an after-work supper.

SERVES 6
YOU WILL NEED: A LIDDED, OVENPROOF CASSEROLE

3 tablespoons olive oil

600g pork tenderloin, cut into chunks

1 onion, finely chopped

2 small leeks, sliced into 1cm pieces

3 garlic cloves, crushed

4–5 sprigs of fresh thyme

1 tablespoon plain flour

2 teaspoons Dijon mustard

1 apple, peeled, cored and cut into small pieces

125ml dry cider or dry white wine

100ml chicken stock

375g sheet of ready-rolled all-butter puff pastry, thawed if frozen

1 small egg, beaten with 1 tablespoon milk

4 tablespoons double cream

a handful of flat-leaf parsley, finely chopped

salt and black pepper

1 Heat the oven to 200°C/400°F/gas 6. Heat half the oil in a flameproof casserole and fry the pork until golden brown all over. Remove with a slotted spoon to a plate and set aside. Add the rest of the oil and fry the onion for 5 minutes before adding the leeks, garlic and thyme and frying gently for a couple more minutes. Add the flour, mustard and apple and mix well together.

2 Add the cider or wine and simmer for a couple of minutes, then add back the browned pork with the stock. Season well and bring to the boil.

3 Meanwhile, unroll the pastry onto a baking sheet and cut into 6 equal squares, then brush with the beaten egg mixture. When the pork mixture is boiling, cover the casserole with a lid and place both the casserole and the baking sheet in the heated oven. Bake for 15–20 minutes until the pork is cooked and the pastry puffed and golden. Stir the cream and parsley into the casserole, spoon onto plates, top with the pastry lids, and serve with mashed potato.

ROB'S GARLIC MUSHROOM ROLLS

These veggie alternatives to sausage rolls come from my love of garlic mushrooms and are a guaranteed way to impress your guests at a dinner party. If you like them extra garlicky, you could throw a few more cloves in. Enjoy with a cheeky mulled wine!

MAKES ABOUT 12

For the filling
30g butter
1 onion, chopped
250g mushrooms, cut into
  1cm cubes, stalks reserved
5 garlic cloves
70g fresh breadcrumbs
a small bunch of fresh flat-leaf
  parsley, chopped

salt and black pepper

For the rough puff pastry
225g plain flour, plus extra
  for dusting
a pinch of salt
140g cold butter, cut into
  1cm cubes
4–6 tablespoons chilled water

1 To make the pastry, sift the flour and salt into a bowl, add the cubes of butter and briefly mix. Using a cutlery knife, stir in enough chilled water to bring the mixture together. Turn out onto a work surface and very briefly knead. Wrap in clingfilm and rest in the fridge for 10 minutes.

2 Roll out the chilled pastry on a lightly floured surface into a long rectangle and fold into thirds, like a letter. Turn the mixture 90 degrees, roll out again and fold into thirds. Wrap in clingfilm and chill in the fridge for 10 minutes, before repeating the rolling and folding process 4 times, with a 10-minute rest in the fridge after each 2 folds. After the last roll and fold, your pastry should have no streaks of butter and is ready to use.

3 Heat the oven to 220°C/425°F/gas 7. Heat half the butter for the filling in a frying pan, add the onion and chopped mushrooms and cook for 3–4 minutes to soften. Set aside to cool.

4 Blend the mushroom stalks with the garlic in a food processor. Add the cooled onion and mushroom mixture and pulse a few times to mix, keeping the mixture chunky. Put into a bowl, add the breadcrumbs, parsley and salt and pepper to taste, and mix together well.

5 Roll out the pastry into a long rectangle, about 40 x 20cm. Spoon the mushroom mixture along the middle of the pastry, using your hands to shape it into a long, thick sausage shape.

6 Melt the remaining butter in a small pan and use to brush down the long edges of the pastry. Bring the bottom edge of the pastry over the mixture and roll into a long sausage shape, so that the seam sits underneath. Cut into 3cm rolls and place on a baking sheet. Brush with melted butter, transfer to the heated oven and bake for 20 minutes (or longer if making larger rolls) until golden brown and puffed up.

HOT-SMOKED SALMON AND DILL RICE FILO PARCELS

This full-of-flavour rice is encased in buttery, crisp pastry and makes a satisfying family supper. Try playing with the ingredients, substituting drained, rinsed capers for cornichons or using hot-smoked mackerel instead of salmon.

MAKES 4

1 tablespoon olive oil
1 banana shallot, finely sliced
150g basmati rice, soaked in cold water for 10 minutes, then rinsed and drained
150g sustainable hot-smoked salmon, flaked

4 spring onions, finely sliced
a small of bunch of fresh dill, finely chopped
grated zest of 1 lemon and a good squeeze of juice
2 heaped tablespoons chopped cornichons

4 tablespoons crème fraîche
12 sheets of filo pastry
75g unsalted butter, melted
salt and black pepper

1 Heat the oil in a pan and gently fry the shallot for 4–5 minutes until softened. Add the rice and stir to coat in the oil, then season with salt and add 300ml water. Cover and bring to the boil, then simmer gently, covered, for 5 minutes. Remove from the heat and leave to stand, still covered, for a further 10 minutes until all the liquid has been absorbed and the rice is lovely and fluffy.

2 Tip the rice into a bowl, fluff up with a fork and allow to cool. Add the salmon, spring onions, dill, lemon zest and juice, cornichons and crème fraîche. Check the seasoning and set aside.

3 Heat the oven to 200°C/400°F/gas 6. Trim the sheets of filo into rectangles about 25 x 22cm. Brush one of the rectangles with melted butter, top with a second rectangle, brush with melted butter, place a third piece of filo on top and brush this last piece with melted butter. Repeat this process to make 4 separate stacks of pastry.

4 Spoon the filling evenly into the centre of the rectangles along the length of the pastry. Brush the edges with melted butter and bring them up to encase the filling; you can do this quite roughly, pressing the pastry together over the top. Brush all over with more melted butter and transfer to a baking sheet.

5 Place in the heated oven and bake for 15–20 minutes until golden and crisp all over. Serve with a winter salad or slaw.

TIP

You need to work quickly with filo pastry, or it becomes dry and brittle. Keep the pastry you aren't working with under a slightly damp tea towel until you are ready to use it.

PARMA HAM, RICOTTA AND MUSHROOM PIZZAS

Homemade pizza may not seem like a quick midweek supper, but in fact it's about as simple as you could wish for. Make the dough as soon as you get home from work, and you will be eating homemade pizza an hour later! Alternatively, whip up the dough in the morning and leave it in the fridge to rise.

MAKES 2 LARGE PIZZAS (SERVES 4)

3 tablespoons olive oil
2 garlic cloves, finely sliced
200g passata
1 tablespoon tomato purée
a few sprigs of fresh oregano
   or thyme, leaves picked
a good knob of butter
200g white mushrooms, sliced
100g ricotta cheese

150g firm mozzarella, sliced
8 slices Parma ham, torn
Parmesan shavings and rocket
   leaves, to serve (optional)
salt and black pepper

For the dough
250g strong white bread flour,
   plus extra for dusting

1½ teaspoons salt
1 x 7g sachet fast-action
   dried yeast
2 teaspoons olive oil, plus
   extra for greasing
150ml warm water

1 To make the dough, sift the flour and salt into a large bowl, then stir in the yeast. Make a well in the centre of the flour and pour in the oil. Add the water to the bowl gradually, mixing with your hands, until it all comes together in a soft dough.

2 Tip onto a lightly floured surface, scraping out any that sticks to the bowl. Knead for 5 minutes until smooth and supple. Put in a lightly oiled bowl, cover with a clean tea towel and leave in a warm place for 1 hour, until doubled in size.

3 To make the sauce, heat 2 tablespoons of the oil in a sauté pan, then gently fry the garlic for 20 seconds. Add the passata, tomato purée and oregano or thyme, then season well. Simmer for 10 minutes or so until reduced to a spreadable sauce, then set aside.

4 Heat the butter and the rest of the oil in a frying pan and fry the mushrooms over a high heat until golden all over. Season and set aside.

5 Heat the oven to its highest temperature with 2 large baking sheets inside. Gently knock the air out of the dough and divide in half. Knead each piece briefly on a lightly floured surface, then, rolling and pulling gently with your hands, stretch out the dough to fit the baking sheets. Don't worry if they are misshapen. Put each base on a sheet of baking paper (which will help transfer them to the oven).

6 Spread each base with 2 tablespoons of the tomato sauce, then scatter with the mushrooms. Dot all over with the ricotta and mozzarella, then add the roughly torn Parma ham.

7 Transfer the pizzas, still on the baking paper, to the heated baking sheets in the oven and bake for 10–12 minutes until the bases are crisp. Scatter with the Parmesan shavings and rocket, if using, and serve immediately.

CATHRYN'S SNOWY WHITE COCONUT TRAYBAKE

This sweet, simple cake is a delicious treat to enjoy with your visitors during the festive season. Or you could make it together with the little ones on a cold, stay-indoors-day during the holidays.

MAKES 16 SLICES
YOU WILL NEED: A 30 X 20CM TIN, GREASED AND LINED

For the cake
150g unsalted butter, softened
250g caster sugar
100ml soured cream
100ml buttermilk
2 eggs and 3 whites
250g self-raising flour
1 teaspoon baking powder
a pinch of salt
75g desiccated coconut

seeds of 5 cardamom pods
(optional), finely ground

For the icing
100g unsalted butter,
softened
200g icing sugar, sifted
2–3 tablespoons soured cream

To decorate
a handful of desiccated coconut

edible white glitter

**For the marshmallow
snowmen (optional)**
strawberry laces
white marshmallows
giant chocolate buttons
round caramel
chocolates
black writing icing

1 Heat the oven to 180°C/350°F/gas 4. Cream the butter and sugar in a large bowl with a hand-held electric whisk or wooden spoon until smooth and pale. Gently whisk together the soured cream, buttermilk, eggs and whites in a separate bowl until just combined. Mix together the dry ingredients in a third bowl.

2 Add the cream and egg mixture and the dry ingredients to the creamed butter and sugar, alternating them a third at a time and whisking after each addition until combined and the mixture is very light and pale. Pour into the prepared tin and gently smooth the top.

3 Place in the middle of the heated oven and bake for 25–30 minutes until lightly golden, and springy to the touch. Turn out onto a wire rack to cool.

4 To make the icing, beat the butter and icing sugar together using an electric beater, for at least 5 minutes, until very light, fluffy and white. Add the soured cream and gently fold through to combine, then beat for a further 1–2 minutes.

5 When the cake is completely cooled, spread the icing over the top, then cut into slices. Alternatively, cut into slices and put the icing into a disposable piping bag, snip off the end and pipe little snowy peaks of icing onto each slice. Finish with a scattering of coconut and glitter, like freshly fallen snow.

6 For the snowmen, cut the strawberry laces into scarves. Spear a cocktail stick through 3 marsh-mallows with the scarf on top of the middle one. Make a hat by pushing a chocolate button and round caramel chocolate onto the top of the cocktail stick. Pipe on icing buttons and a face.

MIRANDA'S CRANBERRY AND PISTACHIO CHOCOLATE CAKES

These rich, fudgy chocolate cupcakes are packed with cranberries, morsels of white chocolate and crunchy pistachio nuts. We love them topped with a simple swirl of milk chocolate ganache. They are perfect for a tea party and make a scrumptious pudding as well! Fun to make with children and you won't be short of volunteers to lick the chocolatey bowls!

MAKES 24
YOU WILL NEED: 2 X 12-HOLE CUPCAKE OR MUFFIN TINS, LINED WITH CUPCAKE CASES

200g milk chocolate, chopped

200g unsalted butter, softened

200g caster sugar

4 medium eggs

300g self-raising flour

50g cocoa powder, sifted

2 teaspoons baking powder

½ teaspoon ground mixed spice (optional)

1 tablespoon milk

150g dried cranberries

125g unsalted shelled pistachio nuts

150g white chocolate, cut into small chunks

For the ganache

200ml double cream

200g milk chocolate, chopped

1 Heat the oven to 180°C/350°F/gas 4.

2 To make the ganache, put the cream and chocolate in a heatproof bowl set over a pan of simmering water, stir to melt and combine, then remove from the heat. (Or place in a microwave, heat for 30-second bursts on high, then remove and stir until melted and combined.) Set aside for about 1 hour, to thicken a little.

3 Melt the chocolate for the cakes in the microwave or in a heatproof bowl set over a pan of simmering water. Set aside to cool a little.

4 Cream together the butter and sugar in a large bowl, using a hand-held electric whisk or wooden spoon, beating well until pale and creamy. Add the melted chocolate and beat again until well combined. Break the eggs into a small bowl and beat with a fork, then add to the mixture a little at a time. Mix until well combined.

5 Gently fold in the flour, cocoa powder, baking powder, mixed spice if using, and milk, then fold in 100g each of the cranberries, pistachios and white chocolate chunks.

6 Spoon into the cupcake cases, only filling each case to just over halfway, to prevent them from overflowing. Place in the heated oven and bake for 18–20 minutes or until springy and firm to touch. Remove from the oven and leave to cool in the tin before removing to a wire rack to cool completely.

7 Use a palette knife or spoon to spread the thickened ganache on top of each cooled cake. Put a little heap of the remaining cranberries, pistachios and white chocolate chunks on top of each cake, while the ganache is still sticky.

MARY'S WHITE CHOCOLATE AND GINGER CHEESECAKE

SERVES 8

YOU WILL NEED: A 20CM ROUND, DEEP-SIDED SPRINGFORM CAKE TIN,
GREASED AND LINED; 1 SMALL PIPING BAG FITTED WITH A SIZE 2 WRITING NOZZLE;
1 LARGE PIPING BAG FITTED WITH A STAR NOZZLE

For the base
50g butter
25g dark chocolate
150g digestive biscuits, crushed

For the filling
300g white chocolate drops,
   or a bar broken into pieces

400g full-fat cream cheese
150ml soured cream
2 eggs
1 teaspoon vanilla extract
4 balls of stem ginger in syrup,
   finely chopped

To decorate
150g dark chocolate, melted
25g marzipan
red food colouring
icing sugar, for dusting
300ml double cream

1 Melt the butter and dark chocolate for the base in a small pan over a low heat. Stir in the crushed biscuits, tip into the prepared tin and press evenly over the base. Chill in the fridge. Meanwhile, heat the oven to 170°C/325°F/gas 3.

2 Put the white chocolate in a heatproof bowl and melt very gently over a pan of hot water (do not allow the chocolate to become too hot), stirring occasionally with a spoon until smooth.

3 Whisk the cream cheese and soured cream together in a large bowl until smooth, then add the eggs and vanilla and whisk until completely smooth with no lumps. Stir in the melted white chocolate and mix together. Fold in the chopped ginger and mix.

4 Pour into the tin and spread evenly over the chilled base. Place in the heated oven and bake for about 45 minutes until firm around the edge and just set in the middle. Remove from the oven and run a small palette knife around the edge of the tin to release, leave to cool, then chill.

5 Meanwhile, for the decoration, spoon the melted chocolate into a small piping bag fitted with a size 2 writing nozzle and pipe 11 small chocolate holly leaves down 2 strips of non-stick baking paper. Place 2 rolling pins on an empty egg box (to prevent them from rolling) and drape the strips of baking paper over the rolling pins, so that the leaves will have a slight curl. (Or you can use 2 rolls of clingfilm or foil and secure with elastic bands on the end.) Leave until set. Colour the marzipan bright red, using the red food colouring. Dust your hands in icing sugar and roll the red marzipan into 27 berries.

6 Remove the outside ring of the tin and lift the base onto a serving plate. Whip the cream to soft peaks and spoon into a piping bag fitted with a star nozzle. Pipe 8 rosettes around the edge of the cheesecake and 1 rosette in the middle. Place 1 chocolate holly leaf and 3 berries on each cream rosette around the edge, and 3 leaves and 3 berries on the cream rosette in the centre, then serve.

PAUL'S MINCE PIES

MAKES 12

YOU WILL NEED: A DEEP 12-HOLE MUFFIN TIN; A 10CM ROUND
PASTRY CUTTER AND AN 8CM FLUTED PASTRY CUTTER

1 x 600g jar of mincemeat

2 tangerines, zest grated and
flesh chopped

1 apple, cored and finely diced

a little milk, for brushing

For the pastry

375g plain flour

250g butter, softened

125g caster sugar, plus extra
for dusting

1 medium egg

a splash of cold water

1 To make the pastry, rub the flour, butter, sugar, egg and splash of cold water together until it just comes together as a dough. Do not overwork it. Wrap in clingfilm and chill in the fridge for at least 30 minutes while you make the filling. Heat the oven to 200°C/400°F/gas 6.

2 Tip the mincemeat into a bowl and add the tangerine zest and flesh, and the diced apple. Mix together using your hand.

3 Roll out the chilled pastry to a 3mm thickness. Using the plain pastry cutter, cut out 12 discs of pastry. Press the discs into the muffin holes and fill each one with a good helping of the mincemeat mixture, to come three-quarters of the way up.

4 Using the fluted pastry cutter, cut out 12 pastry circles for the lids (slightly bigger than the top of the muffin cups). Place a lid on top of each pie and gently push down, then brush each lid with milk.

5 Place in the heated oven and bake for 20 minutes, then transfer to a wire rack to cool. Dust with caster sugar and serve warm, with fresh cream.

GIFTS AND DECORATIONS

GIFTS AND DECORATIONS

Baking is best when it is shared with those close to you and edible gifts are a wonderful present for friends and family.

Biscuits are particularly good gifts: Florentines (page 51) and Almond and Chocolate Biscotti (page 66) taste delicious dipped in tea, or alongside a glass of mulled wine.

For more adventurous bakers, Italy's famous duo of yeasted cakes are ideal gifts, steeped in tradition. Pandori (page 71), whose name comes from 'pan d'oro' or 'golden bread' is traditionally served coated with sugar, to represent snowy peaks, and is perfect for spreading with melted chocolate or dipping in hot cocoa. There are many legends surrounding the richly fruited Panettone (page 75), too. One story describes how the recipe was invented by a rich nobleman who fell in love with the beautiful daughter of a Milanese baker named Toni. To win her love he disguised himself as a baker's apprentice and used his money to buy butter, eggs and fruit, creating this wonderful enriched fruit bread which he called 'Pan di Toni' (Toni's bread) after her father.

Gingerbread is undoubtedly the most popular festive treat, whether it is the treacly German Lebkuchen Stars (page 52) or the lighter ginger-spiced version, cut into festive and fairytale shapes like the Gingerbread House on page 56 – a stunning centrepiece from the Grimm Brothers' classic tale. Using edible decorations in the home dates back to 16th century Germany, where they began to adorn festive pine trees with apples, nuts, marzipan and sugar biscuits like the Stained Glass Tree Biscuits on page 55 – a beautiful, homemade addition to any Christmas tree.

FLORENTINES

These sticky little sweet treats are half biscuit and half chewy caramel goodness.
They have become a classic at Christmas, probably thanks to the candied peel and glacé
cherries that are so beloved at this time of year. Don't worry if they spread into uneven
shapes – it's all part of their homemade charm.

MAKES 16–18

25g unsalted butter
75g caster sugar
2 teaspoons plain flour
4 tablespoons double cream
50g flaked toasted almonds

50g candied peel
25g dried cranberries
25g glacé cherries
100g dark chocolate
100g white chocolate

1 Heat the oven to 190°C/375°F/gas 5 and line 2 baking sheets with non-stick baking paper. Put the butter and sugar into a small pan over a low heat and melt, stirring constantly, until they form a paste. Stir in the flour and cream and heat until you have a smooth batter and the sugar has dissolved. Fold in the almonds, candied peel, cranberries and cherries. Remove from the heat and set aside to cool a little.

2 Spoon small teaspoonfuls of the mixture, well spaced apart, onto one of the lined baking sheets. Bake at the top of the oven for 10–12 minutes until golden, then remove and leave to cool for 2–3 minutes before transferring to a wire rack. Repeat with the second tray.

3 Melt both chocolates in separate bowls set over pans of barely simmering water, making sure the bases of the bowls are not touching the water. Turn the cooled Florentines over so their bases are facing up and use a teaspoon or small palette knife to spread the bases with either white or dark chocolate. Leave to cool completely. If you have any chocolate left you can drizzle the tops of the Florentines with it once the bases are dried.

4 Package into cellophane bags with pretty ribbon or into boxes to give as Christmas gifts.

THINKING AHEAD

These keep well for several weeks, stored in an airtight container in a cool, dry place.

LEBKUCHEN STARS

A classic German Christmas delight, these are a bit like gingerbread, but with a deeper, more treacly and spiced flavour. Make sure you put the icing on when the biscuits are still warm, for the traditional-looking glaze.

〜〜〜〜〜〜〜〜〜〜

MAKES 32
YOU WILL NEED: A 6CM STAR PASTRY CUTTER

60g runny honey
115g black treacle
90g unsalted butter
25g dark muscovado sugar
300g self-raising flour, plus
　　extra for dusting
½ teaspoon bicarbonate
　　of soda
1 teaspoon ground cinnamon
2 teaspoons ground ginger
a good grating of fresh nutmeg

¼ teaspoon ground allspice
a small pinch of ground cloves
a pinch of salt
1 medium egg
finely grated zest of 1 small
　　orange

For the icing
1 medium egg white
150g icing sugar
2 tablespoons lemon juice

〜〜〜〜〜〜〜〜〜〜

1 Melt the honey, treacle, butter and sugar together in a pan, then set aside to cool.

2 Sift the flour, bicarbonate of soda, spices and salt into a bowl and make a well in the centre. Mix the egg and orange zest into the cooled melted butter mixture, then pour this into the well in the dry ingredients. Stir with a wooden spoon until it forms a dough.

3 Turn out onto a lightly floured surface and knead briefly with your hands until smooth, then shape into a disc, wrap well in clingfilm and chill for 30 minutes. Meanwhile, heat the oven to 180°C/350°F/gas 4 and line 2 baking sheets with non-stick baking paper.

4 Roll out the dough on a very lightly floured surface to just over 5mm thick and stamp out stars with the pastry cutter. Place on the baking sheets and re-roll the trimmings to stamp out more. Transfer to the heated oven and bake for 12 minutes. Cool for a minute or two on the baking sheets, then transfer to a wire rack to ice them while still warm.

5 Beat the egg white, icing sugar and lemon juice together to form a paste and brush this onto the still warm cookies. Allow to cool completely.

TIP

This dough freezes brilliantly so if you want to have lebkuchen for yourself as well as for gifts, make double and freeze half, wrapped well in baking paper and clingfilm.

STAINED GLASS TREE BISCUITS

These delicious butter biscuits look fabulous hanging on the tree with the lights catching the stained glass. You will need smaller decorative cutters to make the windows, and a range of flavoured boiled sweets to create different coloured glass.

MAKES 30-35
YOU WILL NEED: CHRISTMAS BISCUIT CUTTERS, ABOUT 8CM;
SMALLER DECORATIVE BISCUIT CUTTERS

12 coloured boiled sweets
125g butter, softened
60g caster sugar
200g plain flour, plus extra
  for dusting

1 teaspoon orange extract
1 tablespoon milk

1 Put the sweets into freezer bags, keeping each colour in a separate bag, and bash with a rolling pin until they break into little pebbles of sugar. Set aside.

2 Using a hand-held electric whisk, beat the butter and sugar together in a bowl, until pale and creamy. Sift in the flour, then add the orange extract and the milk. Use your hands to mix everything together into a ball of dough. Wrap in clingfilm and chill for 10-15 minutes. Meanwhile, heat the oven to 180°C/350°F/gas 4 and line 2 baking sheets with non-stick baking paper.

3 Lightly flour a work surface and roll out half the dough to about 5mm thick. Using the biscuit cutters, cut out shapes and use the smaller decorative cutters to stamp out shapes from the middle of each biscuit. Carefully transfer

the biscuits to the lined baking sheets, using a spatula. Repeat with the remaining dough, and re-roll the trimmings to make more biscuits.

4 Put one good pinch of the crushed sweet pebbles into the middle of each biscuit hole. Place in the heated oven and bake for 15-18 minutes, until the biscuits are just golden and the sweets have melted and filled the cut out areas. Whilst still warm, use a skewer to make holes in the top of each biscuit so you can thread them with string or ribbon to hang on your tree.

5 Leave to cool on the baking sheets until the sweets have set hard, then transfer to a wire rack. Once completely cool, thread with a string or fine ribbon and hang on your tree.

MARY'S GINGERBREAD HOUSE

YOU WILL NEED: 3 LARGE BAKING SHEETS; A STAR PASTRY CUTTER;
2 MEDIUM PIPING BAGS FITTED WITH 2 PLAIN NOZZLES, 1 MEDIUM AND 1 SMALL;
1 X 30CM SQUARE CAKE BOARD; 2 NIGHT-LIGHT CANDLES; 6 COCKTAIL STICKS

375g unsalted butter
300g dark muscovado sugar
150g golden syrup
900g plain flour
1 tablespoon bicarbonate
  of soda
2 tablespoons ground ginger
icing sugar, for dusting

For the icing
3 egg whites
675g icing sugar, sifted
3 teaspoons lemon juice

To decorate
15 yellow or orange boiled sweets
200g giant milk chocolate buttons

1 Heat the oven to 200°C/400°F/gas 6. Melt the butter, sugar and syrup together in a large pan. Sift the flour, bicarbonate of soda and ground ginger together in a large bowl and make a well. Pour in the melted butter mixture, stir it in and, when cool enough to handle, knead to a stiff dough.

2 Divide the mixture into 5 pieces and cut one of these pieces in half (so you have 6 pieces in total). Roll each piece out on a sheet of greaseproof paper to ¾cm thick. Using the templates on pages 246–8, cut out each section and slide, still on the paper, onto 3 baking sheets. Using the template as a guide, a ruler and the rim of a cup, cut out the arched windows on the front and sides of the house. Using the star cutter, cut out a star in the front and back of

the house. Using a knife, cut out the door on the front and back of the house and place the doors separately on the baking sheets.

3 Re-roll the trimmings and use to cut out the chimney and 3 Christmas trees. Place the gingerbread in the heated oven and bake for 7–8 minutes. Meanwhile, crush the boiled sweets to a rough sand texture, using a pestle and mortar. Remove the gingerbread from the oven. Trim the windows if the mixture has spread and sprinkle the crushed sweets into the windows. Return to the oven and continue to cook for 3–4 minutes until the sweets have melted and the gingerbread is firm. Remove from the oven and leave to cool for a few minutes, then trim around the templates again to give clean, sharp edges. Leave to cool completely.

CONTINUED

4 For the icing, whisk the egg whites in a large bowl until frothy. Using a wooden spoon or a hand-held electric mixer on a slow speed, add the icing sugar a tablespoonful at a time. Stir in the lemon juice and beat until it is very stiff and white and stands up in peaks. Cover the surface with a damp cloth if not using immediately.

5 Spoon a little of the icing into a piping bag fitted with a medium plain nozzle, pipe blobs of icing on the back of each chocolate button and stick, overlapping, onto the two roof sections, to create a tile effect on the lower half of the roof. Transfer some icing to a second piping bag, fitted with a small plain nozzle, and pipe frames around the windows, doors and stars, to decorate. Spoon 6 tablespoons of the icing over the cake board and, using a palette knife, spread to cover the board to create a snow effect and a base to attach the house. Pipe some icing along the wall edges and join the house together on the iced cake board. Leave the icing to dry and harden for a minimum of 4 hours, preferably overnight.

6 Place the night-lights inside the house. Cut the pointed ends of the cocktail sticks into 1cm pieces. (You should have 12 small pointed pieces.) Push the blunt end of the cocktail stick pieces into the sloping edges of the front and back of the house, leaving the pointed ends sticking out to act as peg supports to attach the roof. (Remember to remove the sharp cocktail sticks from your gingerbread house before eating it, to avoid a choking hazard.) Pipe icing between the cocktail sticks and fix the 2 roof panels onto the house. Pipe icing around the base and edges of the chimney and attach to the roof.

7 To decorate, spread a layer of icing on the top of the roof sections that is not covered with chocolate buttons, then pipe icing along the apex and edges of the roof to look like snow and icicles. Stick the front door in place with icing. Cut the back door into 3 pieces to use as props to keep the trees upright. Decorate the Christmas trees with piped icing and fix them onto the cake board with icing and gingerbread props. Dust the roof with icing sugar and light the night-lights using a candle lighter through the open back door. Do not leave the candles lit unattended, and it is best not to burn the candles inside the house for longer than 15 minutes or they may singe the inside of the roof and start to melt the chocolate buttons.

SEEDY FLATBREADS FOR CHEESE

These cheese biscuits are easy to make and keep exceptionally well. Experiment with different seeds such as poppy, hemp and chia, or you could try brown mustard seeds, cumin or coriander. Stored in an airtight tin, these will stay crisp for several weeks. Pictured overleaf.

MAKES ABOUT 35, DEPENDING ON SIZE

200g fine polenta
40g milled flaxseed/linseed
40g whole flaxseed/linseed
40g sesame seeds
75g sunflower seeds

75g pumpkin seeds
flaky sea salt
80ml olive oil
450ml boiling water

1 Heat the oven to 150°C/300°F/gas 2 and line 2 large baking sheets with non-stick baking paper. Mix the polenta and seeds together in a bowl. Add a pinch of sea salt and the olive oil and mix well, then add the boiling water and stir with a wooden spoon until it all comes together.

2 Divide the mixture into two and roll out nice and thin between 2 pieces of baking paper, transferring each to a baking sheet on the bottom piece of paper. Score even lines in the mixture to help break it into individual flatbreads later. Scatter with a little more sea salt.

3 Place in the heated oven and bake for 45–50 minutes until golden and crisp. Transfer to a wire rack and leave to cool completely. Once cool, you can break them along the scored lines into individual flatbreads, ready to package up for friends and family.

TIP

If you don't have large baking sheets you can use 3 or 4 smaller ones, or bake in batches, to make sure you get the flatbreads lovely and thin.

HOMEMADE PRETZELS

These are the perfect nibble to accompany a glass of fizz. If you prefer, you can make them sweet rather than savoury by sprinkling them with demerara sugar instead of salt just before baking.

~~~~~~

MAKES 8

175ml warm water
½ teaspoon caster sugar
1 x 7g sachet fast-action
    dried yeast
300g plain flour, plus extra
    for dusting

⅔ teaspoon salt
3 tablespoons bicarbonate
    of soda
1 medium egg, beaten with
    1 tablespoon melted butter
rock salt, for sprinkling

~~~~~~

1 Mix the warm water with the sugar and yeast and leave to stand for 5 minutes until the mixture starts to bubble. Stir together the flour and salt in a bowl. Make a well in the centre, add the yeast mixture and stir until you have a dough.

2 Turn out onto a lightly floured surface and knead for 10 minutes until smooth and elastic. Place the dough in a lightly oiled bowl, cover with a clean tea towel or lightly oiled clingfilm, and leave to rise for 1–2 hours until doubled in size.

3 Heat the oven to 170°C/325°F/gas 3. Put about 1.5 litres water in a large pan with the bicarbonate of soda and bring to the boil.

4 Punch down the risen dough and give it another quick knead. Cut into 8 pieces and roll out each piece to a long, thin rope, about 45–50cm long. You can leave your pretzels as sticks, but if you want to make a classic pretzel shape, take one end of the rope and bring it to the centre. Take the other end of the rope, bring it across the first end and twist it under to form a 'knot' in the centre then bring it to the middle. Press the ends tightly on the top edge of the dough rope to seal them.

5 Lower the shaped pretzels on a slotted spoon into the boiling water – you can do about 3 at a time. Boil for 30 seconds, then remove to a baking sheet lined with non-stick baking paper and repeat with the remaining pretzels.

6 Once all the pretzels have been boiled, brush them with the egg and butter glaze and sprinkle with rock salt. Transfer to the heated oven and bake for 45–50 minutes until dark golden brown and crisp. Cool on a wire rack before eating.

BECA'S STILTON AND FIG SABLÉS

A fantastic gift for the cheese lover at Christmas, these simple yet scrummy and moreish sablés would be a great addition to a hamper alongside some homemade chutney and a bottle of red wine. They also make a great edible gift to take to a drinks party or as part of a canapé selection at home.

MAKES 20–24

YOU WILL NEED: A ROUND 4CM PLAIN PASTRY CUTTER

120g plain flour, plus extra for dusting
80g cold unsalted butter, cut into cubes

100g blue Stilton, chilled, cut into cubes, plus an extra 50g to decorate
a good pinch of salt

80g dried figs, cut into small pieces
1 egg yolk
100g walnuts

1 Put the flour, butter, Stilton and salt into a food processor and pulse until the mixture looks like chunky breadcrumbs (this won't take long, and you don't want the mixture to start to come to together before you've added the remaining ingredients, so keep an eye on things). Add the chopped figs and egg yolk and continue to pulse until the dough comes together into a ball. Alternatively, rub the butter into the flour and salt in a bowl, using your fingertips, then stir in the Stilton, followed by the figs and egg yolk.

2 Tip the dough out onto a lightly floured surface and knead a little, then wrap in clingfilm and chill for at least 20 minutes. Heat the oven to 190°C/375°F/gas 5.

3 Pop the walnuts into a food processor, blitz until ground and spread out on a plate ready to coat the sablés.

4 Remove the chilled dough from the fridge; it should be rested but still pliable. Place between 2 sheets of greaseproof paper and roll out to an 8–10mm thickness. Stamp out the sablés using the pastry cutter and coat in the ground walnuts, before placing on 2 lined baking sheets. Re-roll the trimmings to stamp out the remainder. Cut the 50g Stilton into 1cm cubes and place one on top of each sablé. Transfer to the heated oven and bake for 16–20 minutes, or until golden brown.

5 Leave to cool for a couple of minutes on the baking tray, then transfer to a wire rack to cool completely. Store in an airtight container for up to 5 days, or package them in some greaseproof paper and pretty festive tissue. They can also be packed into cellophane bags and tied with some ribbon, with a label showing the use-by date and storing advice.

THINKING AHEAD

The dough can be made ahead and frozen, defrosted overnight in the fridge before baking, or stored in the fridge for 3–4 days.

ALMOND AND CHOCOLATE BISCOTTI

These hard, nutty little biscuits are begging to be dunked in a cup of black coffee or, better still, a lovely glass of vin santo.

MAKES 45–50

200g whole almonds (skin on)
450g plain flour, plus extra
    for dusting
1 teaspoon baking powder
a good pinch of salt

300g caster sugar
200g dark chocolate chips
3 large eggs and 2 large yolks
1 teaspoon vanilla extract

1 Heat the oven to 180°C/350°F/gas 4 and line 2 baking sheets with non-stick baking paper. Spread the almonds out on one of the baking sheets and toast in the oven for 10 minutes, until lightly golden. Remove and cool.

2 Put the flour, baking powder and salt into a mixing bowl and stir in the sugar, roasted almonds and chocolate chips.

3 In a jug, lightly beat the eggs and extra yolks with the vanilla extract. Make a well in the centre of the dry ingredients and stir in the egg mixture until it comes together into a soft dough. Turn out onto a lightly floured surface and knead briefly until smooth.

4 Divide the dough into 3 and roll each piece into a long sausage, about 4–5cm thick. Transfer to the lined baking sheets and bake for 25–30 minutes, until lightly golden and cooked, so that a skewer inserted into the centre comes out clean. Remove from the oven and cool for at least 10 minutes. Reduce the oven temperature to 150°C/300°F/gas 2.

5 Using a sharp, serrated knife, cut each log slightly on the diagonal into slices approximately 1.5cm thick. Place the biscotti, cut sides down, on the baking sheets and bake for a further 20 minutes, turning the biscotti over halfway through.

6 Transfer to a wire rack and leave to cool completely. The biscotti will become harder as they cool. Once cold, they are ready to package up for gifts.

TIP

You can vary the flavour of your biscotti: try using hazelnuts instead of almonds or adding orange or coffee extract instead of vanilla.

THINKING AHEAD

These biscuits keep for weeks stored in an airtight container.

MINI WALNUT AND FRUIT LOAVES

Perfect as individual place settings, mini loaves make great little treats
for your guests. Wrap each one individually in its tin and leave on
the plate to enjoy with a wedge of Stilton. Pictured overleaf.

MAKES 12 MINI LOAVES
YOU WILL NEED: 12 MINI 150G LOAF TINS, 9 X 6 X 4CM, GREASED AND FLOURED (OR SEE TIP)

400g strong white bread flour,
plus extra for dusting
100g strong wholemeal flour
1 x 7g sachet fast-action
dried yeast

1 teaspoon salt
275–295ml lukewarm water
75g sultanas
75g walnut pieces, chopped

1 Mix the flours, yeast and salt in a bowl and
make a well in the centre. Add enough of the
water to bring it together into a soft dough.

2 Turn out onto a lightly floured surface and
knead for 5 minutes until smooth and elastic.
Place the dough in a clean bowl, cover with
a clean tea towel and leave to rise in a warm
place for about 1 hour or until doubled in size.

3 Knock back the dough using your hands and
knead in the sultanas and chopped walnuts.
Divide the dough into 12 pieces (each weighing
about 80g), shape into small ovals and place
in the prepared mini loaf tins. Place the tins
on a baking sheet, cover again and leave in
a warm place for about 30–40 minutes, until
doubled in size. Meanwhile, heat the oven
to 200°C/400°F/gas 6.

4 Brush the risen loaves with a little water
and sprinkle with a little white flour. Place the
tins, on the baking sheet, in the heated oven
and bake for 20-25 minutes until well risen and
golden, and they sound hollow when you tap
them on the base. Turn out onto a wire rack
and leave to cool completely.

5 Once cool, package them up to give as gifts
along with some seasonal British cheeses and
chutney. Eat within 3 days, or freeze.

TIP

If you don't have mini loaf tins, you can bake
these as freeform loaves without tins. Use your
hands to shape each loaf into an oval or mini
bloomer shape, and slash the top of the risen
shaped loaves with 3 small slashes to help
control the direction they rise in. Or you can
make 2 larger loaves if you prefer.

KIMBERLEY'S BABÀ AL LIMONCELLO

THE GREAT
BRITISH BAKE OFF
KIMBERLEY WILSON
2013

These light, syrup-soaked sponges make delicious, unique edible gifts. All the hard work is done in a mixer so they are surprisingly easy to make.

MAKES 48 MINI BABÀS
YOU WILL NEED: 2 X 12-HOLE MINI MUFFIN TRAYS, BRUSHED WITH MELTED BUTTER; 7–8 WIDE-NECKED 300G JARS, STERILISED

For the dough
350g plain flour
a pinch of salt
finely grated zest of 1 orange
4 large eggs
2 teaspoons fast-action
 dried yeast
2 tablespoons runny honey
125g unsalted butter, softened

For the syrup
1 litre water
1kg granulated sugar
1 vanilla pod, slit in half
 lengthways
2 pared strips of lemon zest
400ml lemon juice
400ml limoncello
2 tablespoons dried lavender
 leaves (optional)
vanilla cream, to serve
 (optional)

1 Put the flour, salt and orange zest into the bowl of a mixer fitted with a whisk or dough hook attachment. Stir to distribute the orange zest.

2 Whisk together the eggs, yeast and honey in a large jug. Turn the mixer onto a medium speed and slowly pour in the egg mixture until you have a soft dough. You may need to scrape the sides of the bowl halfway through. Add the butter 1 teaspoon at a time until it is fully incorporated.

3 Add 1 teaspoon of the mixture to each buttered muffin cup. Cover with lightly buttered clingfilm and leave to rise until the dough reaches the top of the tray, about 1 hour. Meanwhile, heat the oven to 180°C/350°F/gas 4.

4 To make the syrup, heat the water and sugar in a pan over a medium heat until the sugar dissolves. Add the vanilla pod, lemon zest and juice, increase the heat and boil for 3–4 minutes. Add the limoncello and lavender, if using, and boil for a further 1 minute then remove from the heat and allow to cool. It is important that the syrup is not too hot when you come to soak the babàs as it will make the dough disintegrate. When it is ready it should feel warm to the touch. Remove the vanilla pod and lemon zest.

5 Place the risen babàs in the heated oven and bake for 12–15 minutes until golden brown. Cool for a couple of minutes in the trays before removing to a wire rack to cool completely.

6 Submerge the cooled babàs, a few at a time, in the warm syrup for 20–30 seconds, then place on a plate. To serve immediately, halve each babà and fill with whipped vanilla cream then drizzle with the syrup.

7 To present the babàs as a gift, arrange them closely but not tightly in the jar. Fill all the jars with babàs and then top up with the syrup. Seal tightly. Decorate the jars with handwritten tags, and store in a cool, dark place until you give them. They keep for around 3–4 days.

CHOCOLATE AND VANILLA BUTTON BISCUITS

Here are some deliciously simple butter biscuits that make a pretty gift. Play around with different shapes and designs: take a look at buttons on your clothes, or look online at vintage buttons to get ideas.

MAKES 18–20

YOU WILL NEED: 4–6CM PLAIN AND FLUTED PASTRY CUTTERS

145g plain flour

75g icing sugar

½ teaspoon baking powder

100g butter, softened

2 medium egg yolks

1 teaspoon vanilla extract

12g cocoa powder

1 In a bowl, mix the flour, icing sugar and baking powder together. Add the butter and, with your fingertips, rub into the flour until it forms a sandy mixture. Add the egg yolks and quickly mix into a dough. Divide in half, then add the vanilla to one half and the cocoa powder to the other half. Knead both separately until smooth.

2 Roll out each dough half separately between 2 sheets of baking paper and chill in the fridge for 15 minutes. Meanwhile, heat the oven to 180°C/350°F/gas 4 and line 2 baking sheets with non-stick baking paper.

3 Use the pastry cutters to make your button shapes, and place on the lined baking sheets. Re-roll the trimmings to make as many biscuits as possible.

4 Use an egg cup or similar to score indentations inside the rim of the biscuits. Use a small straw or icing nozzle to cut out holes in the centre of your

buttons, some with 2 holes and some with 4, playing around with different utensils to make patterns and indentations on the dough (see introducton). If the dough starts to soften, chill for 10 minutes.

5 Place in the heated oven and bake for 10–12 minutes. Leave to cool for 10 minutes on the baking sheets before transferring to a wire rack to cool completely.

THINKING AHEAD

The uncooked dough freezes well, wrapped in non-stick baking paper and clingfilm. Defrost before rolling it out.

PAUL'S PANETTONE

YOU WILL NEED: AN ELECTRIC MIXER WITH DOUGH HOOK, AN 18CM PANETTONE TIN

500g strong white bread flour
7g salt
50g caster sugar
2 x 7g sachets fast-action
  dried yeast
140ml warm milk
5 medium eggs

250g unsalted butter,
  softened, plus extra, melted,
  for greasing
120g dried cherries
120g dried sultanas
120g dried currants
100g whole blanched almonds

1 Put the flour, salt, sugar, yeast, milk and the eggs in the bowl of an electric mixer fitted with a dough hook. Begin by mixing slowly on number 2 for 2 minutes, then move up to number 4 and mix for a further 6-8 minutes until you have a soft dough.

2 Add the softened butter and mix for another 4-5 minutes, scraping down the bowl from time to time. The dough will be very soft. Add the dried fruit and nuts and mix until it is all incorporated. Tip the dough into a bowl, cover and chill overnight or for 7 hours, until the dough has hardened and you are able to shape it.

3 Prepare the panettone tin by brushing the insides with melted butter, using the pastry brush in an upward motion. Chill until set, then repeat.

4 Remove the dough from the fridge, knock back, shape into a ball and place in the buttered tin. Leave to prove in the fridge for a further 6 hours.

5 Heat the oven to 190°C/375°F/gas 5. When the panettone is risen, place in the heated oven and bake for 20-25 minutes or until a skewer comes out clean, bearing in mind that the sugar and butter in the dough will make it take on colour before it is fully baked. Remove the panettone from the tin and allow to cool.

COME ON
OVER

COME ON OVER

For many, Christmas is a time for large gatherings and get-togethers.

Even for those who would rather keep it small, there are days around this time of year when a few bakes and dishes in the freezer are just what you need when friends and family descend.

These are recipes and ideas to make your life easier. All can be frozen or made in advance, and can be on the table with the minimum of fuss. You will find everything from simple and comforting dishes such as the Best-Ever Shepherd's Pie (page 80) and seasonal gratins and bakes (pages 87 and 83), to showstopping mains that can't fail to impress, like Salmon Wellington wrapped in a delicate brioche crust (page 88).

Keep things Christmassy with some classic sweet bakes such as Stollen (page 94), a sweet and fruited bread rolled with almond paste. This has been a festive staple in Germany since the 1400s, when it was said to represent the baby Jesus wrapped in swaddling. If you aren't a fan of marzipan and icing, a Genoa Cake (page 97) is the perfect fruit cake to enjoy over Christmas instead of the classically iced cake.

You can never have too many mince pies and the frangipane topped Alternative Mince Pies on page 99 are particularly moreish thanks to the very delicate pastry, which uses a little lard in the mix to make it extra short and crumbly. And don't forget, if it's your first mince pie of the season, it's traditional to make a wish!

BEST-EVER SHEPHERD'S PIE

Shepherd's pie is the ultimate comfort food: simple and pleasing, and full of flavour.
If you can't find mushroom ketchup, just fry a few finely chopped chestnut mushrooms
with the onion, and add a little more Worcestershire sauce.

SERVES 4
YOU WILL NEED: A 1.2 LITRE OVENPROOF DISH

6 medium potatoes, peeled
and cut into chunks
a good knob of butter, plus
extra for the topping
2 tablespoons double cream
2 tablespoons olive oil
1 large onion, finely sliced
500g lamb mince
1 teaspoon English mustard
powder

3 tablespoons tomato purée
2–3 tablespoons
Worcestershire sauce
1 tablespoon mushroom
ketchup
2–3 tablespoons tomato
ketchup
75–100ml chicken stock
20g Cheddar cheese, grated
salt and black pepper

1 Bring the potatoes to the boil in a pan of cold, salted water, then turn down and simmer for 20 minutes until very tender. Drain and mash well with the butter and cream. Taste and adjust the seasoning.

2 Meanwhile, heat the oil in a pan and gently fry the onion over a low heat for 10 minutes until softened. Add the lamb mince, increase the heat and fry, stirring to break up the mince, until browned all over.

3 Stir in the mustard powder, tomato purée, Worcestershire sauce and the mushroom and tomato ketchups. Add enough stock to make the mixture moist and juicy, season with a little salt and pepper and simmer for 30 minutes. Meanwhile, heat the oven to 200°C/400°F/gas 6.

4 Spoon the mince into an ovenproof dish and top with the mash. Scatter the cheese over the top and dot with extra butter. Place in the heated oven and bake for 25–30 minutes until golden brown and piping hot.

TIP

For cottage pie, use beef mince instead of lamb.

THINKING AHEAD

Freeze the assembled, unbaked pie until solid, then wrap in foil and freeze for up to 3 months. Bake from frozen, adding 15–20 minutes to the cooking time.

DEEP CHEESE AND BACON TART WITH WHOLEMEAL PASTRY

The wholemeal flour in this pastry adds a lovely nutty flavour, but makes it a little stiffer to work with than a simple shortcrust pastry so it may take a bit more water to bring it together.

SERVES 8–10
YOU WILL NEED: A 23CM ROUND, LOOSE-BOTTOMED CAKE TIN

2 tablespoons olive oil
250g smoked bacon lardons
1 large onion, roughly chopped
6 large eggs, lightly beaten
200ml double cream
100ml soured cream
1 tablespoon Dijon mustard
100g Cheddar cheese, grated
75g Caerphilly, Cheshire or
Wensleydale cheese, finely crumbled
a handful of fresh flat-leaf parsley, finely chopped
salt and black pepper

For the pastry
300g plain flour, plus extra for dusting
175g wholemeal flour
½ teaspoon salt
225g cold unsalted butter, cut into cubes
1 large egg yolk
3–4 tablespoons ice-cold water

1 To make the pastry, put both flours with the salt in a food processor and pulse to combine. Add the butter and pulse until it resembles breadcrumbs. (You can do this by hand, rubbing in the butter, if you prefer.)

2 Add the egg yolk and pulse (or mix with a flat-bladed knife), gradually adding enough chilled water for the mixture to just come together. Tip out onto a lightly floured surface, bring it together with your hands and briefly knead. Shape into a disc, wrap in clingfilm and chill for 15 minutes.

3 Roll the chilled pastry out on a lightly floured surface and use to line the cake tin. Trim any excess pastry, prick the base all over with a fork and chill for 30 minutes. Meanwhile, heat the oven to 220°C/425°F/gas 7 and put in a baking sheet to heat up.

4 Line the pastry case with baking paper and fill with ceramic baking beans or rice, place on the hot baking sheet and blind bake for 15 minutes, then remove the paper and beans and bake for a further 5–10 minutes until crisp and golden. Remove from the oven and reduce the temperature to 180°C/350°F/gas 4.

5 Meanwhile, heat the oil in a frying pan over a low heat and fry the bacon for 4–5 minutes, until golden and crisp. Remove with a slotted spoon and set aside. Add the onion to the pan and fry gently for 10 minutes. Remove with a slotted spoon and add to the bacon. Allow to cool.

6 Mix the eggs, cream, soured cream, mustard, cheeses and parsley in a bowl, and season well. Stir in the cooled bacon and onions, then pour the filling into the baked pastry case. Place in the oven and bake for 50–55 minutes, until golden brown and just set in the middle; if it is browning too quickly, cover it with foil. Remove from the oven and allow to cool for 10 minutes before removing from the tin.

BEEF AND BEER PIE

Beef and beer is a classic combination. The rich, hoppy flavour of the beer mellows on cooking as it mingles with the other ingredients. Beef shin is great for this dish as it becomes so tender, but you could use any cut suitable for slow cooking, such as cheek or braising steak. Pictured overleaf.

SERVES 6
YOU WILL NEED: A LARGE OVENPROOF CASSEROLE; A 2 LITRE PIE DISH

1.5kg beef shin, cut into large pieces
2 tablespoons plain flour, seasoned with salt and pepper
vegetable oil or dripping, for frying
250g smoked bacon lardons
1 large onion, finely chopped
500ml ale

500ml good quality beef stock
1 tablespoon light muscovado sugar
2 teaspoons red wine vinegar
1 tablespoon Dijon mustard
4–5 sprigs of fresh rosemary
2 bay leaves
30g unsalted butter
200g small shallots, peeled

200g button mushrooms
milk, for brushing

For the pastry
250g plain flour, plus extra for dusting
½ teaspoon baking powder
a good pinch of salt
100g beef suet
a little cold water

1 Heat the oven to 170°C/325°F/gas 3. Dust the beef in the seasoned flour. Heat a layer of oil in a large non-stick frying pan and brown the beef in batches, transferring it to a large casserole.

2 Heat a little more oil in the frying pan and fry the bacon until golden and crisp, then add it to the casserole using a slotted spoon. Fry the onion in the bacon fat for 5 minutes until softened, then add to the casserole.

3 Pour the ale and stock over the meat and then add the sugar, vinegar, mustard and herbs. Bring to the boil, season well and cover with a lid. Transfer to the heated oven and bake for 2½–3 hours until the meat is tender and starting to fall apart. If the sauce is still very runny, remove the meat with a slotted spoon and boil the sauce down until it has a lovely coating consistency. Check the seasoning and set aside to cool.

4 To make the pastry, put all the dry ingredients into a bowl and mix well. Add enough cold water to bring it together to a soft, but not wet, dough. Knead briefly until smooth.

5 Turn the oven up to 190°C/375°F/gas 5. Melt the butter with a little more oil in a pan and fry the shallots until golden brown. Add to the pie filling and do the same with the mushrooms. Spoon all the pie filling into the pie dish. Roll the pastry out on a lightly floured surface and cover the pie, pressing the edges with your fingers to form a good seal. Cut a small steam hole in the centre and brush all over with milk.

6 Place in the heated oven and bake for 50 minutes until golden brown all over.

THINKING AHEAD

Make and cool the filling, then either freeze in a container and defrost to finish the recipe or spoon it into the pie dish, top with pastry and freeze as a whole. Cook from frozen, adding an extra 20–30 minutes to the cooking time.

CHICKEN, SAGE AND CHESTNUT GRATIN

A gratin is a great crowd-pleaser and this one ticks all the boxes: a rich and creamy filling topped with a golden crispy crumb – all you need is a green salad or peas and you are ready to go.

SERVES 4-6
YOU WILL NEED: A 2 LITRE OVENPROOF DISH

4 chicken legs and 2 breasts
2 onions, 1 roughly chopped and 1 finely chopped
2 celery sticks, chopped
1 carrot, chopped
2 bay leaves
10 black peppercorns
2 tablespoons olive oil

50g butter
200g cooked peeled chestnuts, roughly chopped
2 teaspoons fennel seeds
30g plain flour
150ml white wine
4 tablespoons crème fraîche

a handful of fresh sage leaves, chopped
a small bunch of fresh flat-leaf parsley, chopped
75g ciabatta bread, roughly torn into pieces
salt and black pepper

1 Put all the chicken pieces in a large saucepan with the roughly chopped onion, the celery, carrot, bay leaves and peppercorns. Cover with cold water and bring to the boil. Turn down the heat and simmer for 20–25 minutes until the chicken is cooked.

2 Remove the chicken with a slotted spoon and set aside until cool enough to handle. Remove all the meat from the legs, reserving the bones, and shred into bite-sized pieces. Slice the breasts, removing and discarding the skin.

3 Strain the chicken cooking liquid and measure out 1 litre into a separate pan. Add the bones and bubble away until it has reduced by half, then strain again. Heat the oven to 200°C/400°F/gas 6.

4 Heat 1 tablespoon of the oil with the butter in a large pan over a medium heat. Add the finely chopped onion and fry for 5 minutes until soft. Add the chestnuts and fennel seeds and fry for 1 minute, then stir in the flour and cook for

1 further minute. Add the wine and bubble for 1 minute, then gradually add the reduced stock and the shredded chicken. Season well and add the crème fraîche and herbs.

5 Spoon evenly into the dish. Scatter with the ciabatta pieces, season, then drizzle with the remaining oil. Place in the heated oven and bake for 20 minutes until golden and bubbling hot.

TIP

This would also be a great recipe for using up leftover turkey meat – use about 700g cooked white and brown turkey meat instead of the chicken legs and breast, and 500ml good stock.

THINKING AHEAD

Freeze the finished dish, wrapped well in foil, then defrost and reheat in a medium oven when hungry hordes descend.

SALMON WELLINGTON

This uses a brioche dough as a crust, which is amazingly malleable and keeps the fish so tender and juicy. You can either start this recipe the night before or very early in the morning before you want to cook your Wellington.

SERVES 6–8

250g baby spinach
220g watercress
a good grating of nutmeg
200g white crab meat
2 tablespoons mayonnaise
a small bunch of fresh dill, finely chopped
a good squeeze of lemon juice
1.5kg sustainable salmon fillet, skinned and cut into two pieces
1 small egg, beaten with a little milk

salt and black pepper

For the dough
12g fresh yeast OR 1 x 7g sachet fast-action dried yeast
4 tablespoons lukewarm water
300g plain flour, plus extra for dusting
½ teaspoon salt
3 medium eggs, lightly beaten
100g butter, softened

1 To make the dough, mix the yeast with the water and set aside for a few minutes until it starts to bubble, then add to 65g of the flour and mix well. Set aside for 20 minutes to become frothy and double in volume.

2 Mix the remaining flour and salt in a bowl and make a well in the centre. Add the yeast and flour mixture and the beaten eggs and beat together with a wooden spoon. Add the softened butter and mix with your hands until smooth, soft and shiny. Cover with a clean tea towel and leave in a warm place for 1½ hours or until doubled in size. (You can at this point cover it with lightly greased clingfilm and chill in the fridge overnight, which will make it more manageable.)

3 Wilt the spinach and watercress in a pan with a little splash of water. Once wilted, cool quickly under cold running water, then squeeze as much liquid as you can from the leaves. You may want to use some kitchen paper to really dry it. Finely chop and season with nutmeg, salt and pepper.

4 Mix the crab meat with the mayonnaise, dill and lemon juice. Season lightly and mix with the watercress and spinach.

5 Heat the oven to 180°C/350°F/gas 4, with a baking sheet inside. Roll the dough out on a floured surface to a 45 x 29cm rectangle. Transfer to a large sheet of non-stick baking paper.

6 Place one of the salmon pieces in the centre of the dough, with what would have been the skin side down. Top evenly with two-thirds of the crab mixture. Place the other salmon fillet on top, with what would have been skin side up. Top with the remaining crab and watercress mixture. Brush the exposed pastry with the

CONTINUED

beaten egg mixture, bring the pastry up and over the salmon and press to seal.

7 Brush all over with the beaten egg mixture and score a diamond pattern with the tip of a sharp knife. Transfer, on the paper, to the hot baking sheet in the heated oven. Bake for 40–45 minutes until golden brown, then remove from the oven and leave to stand for 5–10 minutes before serving.

TIP

You want to have your two pieces of salmon as evenly sized as possible. You can cut a single fillet in half but you will find one half is thinner and therefore cooks faster. Ask your fishmonger to cut you two 750g pieces from the thick end of two sides of salmon to make them as even as possible.

THINKING AHEAD

Freeze the assembled, unglazed Wellington on a baking sheet for an hour or two until solid, then wrap well in baking paper and clingfilm or foil and freeze for up to 1 month. Glaze and cook from frozen, adding an extra 15–20 minutes to the cooking time.

RICH PUMPKIN, CHILLI, CHARD AND FETA PARCELS

This hearty mix of winter vegetables will delight carnivores and vegetarians alike. Chard is a robust leafy green and the stems add texture and substance to the finished dish, but if you can't find it, use wilted spinach instead.

MAKES 8

50g unsalted butter
1 tablespoon olive oil
1 red onion, finely sliced
2 garlic cloves, crushed
1 red chilli, finely chopped
600g pumpkin, peeled and cut into 1cm chunks

10–12 fresh sage leaves, finely chopped
a splash of vegetable stock
300g green or ruby chard, finely sliced
500g block of all-butter puff pastry, thawed if frozen

plain flour, for dusting
200g feta cheese, cubed
a good squeeze of lemon juice
1 small egg, beaten with a little water
1 tablespoon sesame seeds
salt and black pepper

1 Melt the butter in a frying pan with the olive oil, then add the onion and fry for 5 minutes. Add the garlic, chilli, pumpkin, sage and stock and cook, covered, for 10–15 minutes until the pumpkin is just tender. Set aside to cool completely.

2 Blanch the chard in boiling water for 30 seconds, then drain and refresh under cold water. Squeeze out any excess water and mix with the cooled pumpkin.

3 Meanwhile, cut the pastry in half and roll out each half on a lightly floured surface to roughly a 28cm square. Cut each into 4 equal squares, place all 8 on 2 baking sheets and chill for 10 minutes. Heat the oven to 200°C/400°F/gas 6.

4 Add the feta and lemon juice to the pumpkin and chard mix and season well. Divide between the middle of the pastry squares. Fold a corner of pastry into the middle, then the opposite corner to meet it. Press together to seal. Do the same with the other corners, then press all the sides together to seal. Repeat with the remaining squares of pastry. Brush all over the tops with the beaten egg and scatter with sesame seeds.

5 Place in the heated oven and bake for 20–25 minutes until golden brown, then remove and allow to cool for 10 minutes before serving.

THINKING AHEAD

Freeze the assembled, unglazed parcels on a baking sheet for a couple of hours until solid, then place in a large container between layers of greaseproof paper and freeze for up to 2 months. Glaze, top and cook from frozen, adding an extra 10–15 minutes to the cooking time.

CARAMELISED ONION AND STILTON TART

Few things can beat a homemade caramelised onion tart, so keep any accompaniment simple. The key is leaving time for the onions to become really sticky and golden. With a touch of cheese and herbs rounding out the onion's sweetness, this tart makes a delicious supper. You can swap thyme or oregano for the rosemary and use any cheese you like.

SERVES 8
YOU WILL NEED: A 23CM FLUTED, DEEP TART TIN

2 tablespoons olive oil
45g butter
3 large Spanish onions, finely sliced
a sprig of fresh rosemary, leaves stripped and finely chopped
2 medium eggs and 1 yolk
300ml double cream
50g Parmesan cheese, finely grated
100g Stilton cheese, crumbled
50g toasted pine nuts
salt and black pepper

For the pastry
200g plain flour, plus extra for dusting
½ teaspoon salt
125g cold unsalted butter, diced
1 medium egg yolk
1–2 tablespoons iced water

1 For the pastry, put the flour and salt in a bowl. Add the butter and rub in with your fingertips until it is the texture of fine breadcrumbs. Stir through the egg yolk and enough iced water for the pastry to just start to come together. Knead lightly, then shape into a disc, wrap in clingfilm and chill for 30 minutes.

2 Meanwhile, heat the oil and butter in a large frying pan. Add the onions and rosemary, season, cover and cook over a low heat for 30–40 minutes until very soft. Remove the lid and cook for 15–20 minutes to evaporate the liquid and until the onions start to caramelise. Set aside to cool.

3 Roll out the pastry on a lightly floured surface and line the tart tin. Prick the base all over and chill for 20 minutes. Heat the oven with a baking sheet inside to 200°C/400°F/gas 6.

4 Line the pastry case with baking paper, fill with ceramic baking beans or rice and blind bake for 12 minutes. Remove the paper and beans, then return the tin to the heated oven for a further 5 minutes. Remove from the oven and turn the temperature down to 180°C/350°F/gas 4.

5 Mix the eggs and yolk with the cream and cheeses, and season well. Fold the pine nuts through the onions and spoon over the base of the tart, then pour over the cheese and cream mixture. Place in the heated oven and bake for 30–35 minutes until just set. Allow to cool for 10 minutes before removing from the tin and serving.

PAUL'S STOLLEN

SERVES 10–12

MAKES 1 LARGE OR 2 MEDIUM-SIZED LOAVES

500g strong white bread flour,
  plus extra for dusting

100g caster sugar

10g fast-action dried yeast

10g salt

150g unsalted butter,
  softened, plus 50g, melted

250ml full-fat milk

a pinch of ground nutmeg

a pinch of ground cloves

½ teaspoon vanilla extract

2 drops of almond extract

55g blanched almonds,
  finely chopped

200g raisins

100g currants

125g mixed peel

225g natural marzipan

2 tablespoons icing sugar,
  sifted

1 Put the flour and sugar in a large bowl. Add the yeast on one side of the bowl and the salt on the other. Add the softened butter and 200ml of the milk and stir together. Add the remaining milk and knead well on a generously floured surface for 6–7 minutes, until smooth and pliable.

2 Mix the nutmeg, cloves, vanilla and almond extracts, chopped almonds, dried fruit and mixed peel together in a bowl. Add the dough on top and knead from the outside into the centre. When everything has been fully incorporated, return to the bowl, cover with clingfilm and leave to rise for 1–2 hours in a warm place, until doubled in size.

3 Flatten the dough and roll out on a lightly floured surface to a rectangle about 45 x 35cm. Brush with half of the melted butter. Roll out the marzipan to about 25 x 15cm and place on top of the dough. Starting from a long side, roll the dough up to enclose the marzipan and transfer to a lined baking sheet. Cover and leave to rise for 45 minutes–1 hour until risen and doubled in size.

4 Meanwhile, heat the oven to 190°C/375°F/gas 5. Place the risen stollen in the oven and bake for 1 hour. Remove from the oven, brush with the remaining melted butter and dust with icing sugar. Serve cold.

JAMAICAN GINGERBREAD LOAF

Intensely dark from the addition of ginger and treacle, this warm, spicy cake
is ideal for a cold winter's day when the snow is falling or the rain is lashing.

MAKES 1 LOAF, 8–10 SLICES
YOU WILL NEED: A 450G LOAF TIN, GREASED AND LINED

100g golden syrup
100g black treacle
100g unsalted butter
100g dark muscovado sugar
175g plain flour
½ teaspoon bicarbonate
   of soda

1 tablespoon ground ginger
1 teaspoon ground mixed
   spice
1 large egg
100g stem ginger in syrup,
   chopped
100ml full-fat milk

1 Heat the oven to 170°C/325°F/gas 3. Put the syrup, treacle, butter and sugar in a pan over a low heat and cook until the butter has melted and the sugar dissolved. Set aside.

2 Put the flour, bicarbonate of soda and ground spices in a bowl. Make a well in the centre and add the butter mixture, the egg, chopped stem ginger and milk. Mix with a wooden spoon to form a batter.

3 Pour into the prepared tin, place in the heated oven and bake for 50–60 minutes or until the cake is firm to the touch and a skewer inserted into the centre comes out clean. Leave to cool in the tin for 10 minutes, then turn out onto a wire rack to cool completely.

THINKING AHEAD

Once cold you can eat the loaf straight away, but it will taste better if you can resist for 2–3 days. Wrap well in baking paper and foil and store in a cool, dark place to allow the flavours to mellow and the cake to become lovely and sticky. If you want to make it further in advance, wrap the cooled cake in baking paper and foil or clingfilm and freeze. Defrost at room temperature.

MARY'S CHRISTMAS GENOA CAKE

MAKES 1 CAKE
**YOU WILL NEED: A 23CM ROUND, DEEP CAKE TIN, GREASED AND LINED
WITH A DOUBLE LAYER OF NON-STICK BAKING PAPER; COLOURED RIBBON**

350g red or natural glacé cherries

1 x 225g tin of pineapple in natural juice

50g ready-to-eat dried apricots

100g blanched almonds

finely grated zest of 2 lemons

350g sultanas

250g unsalted butter, softened

250g caster sugar

5 large eggs, lightly beaten

250g self-raising flour

75g ground almonds

To decorate

blanched whole almonds

walnut halves

red or natural glacé cherries, halved

50g whole crystallised orange peel (available in health food shops)

100g apricot jam

1 Heat the oven to 170°C/325°F/gas 3.

2 Cut the glacé cherries into quarters, put in a sieve, rinse under cold running water, then drain well. Drain and roughly chop the pineapple, then dry the pineapple and cherries very thoroughly on kitchen paper. Snip the dried apricots into pieces and roughly chop the almonds. Place the prepared fruits and nuts in a bowl with the lemon zest and sultanas, and gently mix together.

3 Cream the butter and sugar together in a food mixer, or using a hand-held electric whisk, until light and fluffy. Add the eggs a little at a time, alternating with a spoonful of flour to prevent the mixture curdling. Fold in the flour and ground almonds, then lightly fold in the fruit and nuts. Turn the mixture into the prepared cake tin.

Level the surface and decorate the top with the blanched whole almonds, walnut halves, halved glacé cherries and pieces of orange peel.

4 Place in the heated oven and bake for about 2¼ hours or until golden brown, covering the cake loosely with foil after 1 hour to prevent the top becoming too dark. When cooked, a skewer inserted into the centre of the cake should come out clean.

5 Leave to cool in the tin for 30 minutes, then turn out, peel off the baking paper and finish cooling on a wire rack. Warm the apricot jam in a small pan over a low heat, then sieve it. Brush the warm sieved jam over the top of the cooled cake and wrap the ribbon around the edge.

FRANGIPANE MINCE PIES

Mince pies are the very essence of Christmas, and these are a far cry from the typical solid, shortbready, shop-bought varieties. There is no shame in using a jar of mincemeat, or even, if you are short of time, some ready-made shortcrust pastry. The soft frangipane topping elevates these from humble mince pies to showstoppers.

MAKES 24
YOU WILL NEED: A 7.5CM FLUTED PASTRY CUTTER; 2 X 12-HOLE BUN TINS

For the pastry
300g plain flour, plus extra
  for dusting
a pinch of salt
135g cold unsalted butter,
  cut into cubes
55g lard, cut into cubes
2–3 tablespoons ice-cold water

For the frangipane
130g butter, softened
130g caster sugar
2 medium eggs
2 teaspoons dark rum
2 tablespoons plain flour
150g ground almonds

1 x 400g jar of mincemeat
icing sugar, for dusting

1 For the pastry, put the flour and salt into a large bowl and, using your fingers, gently rub in the butter and lard until it resembles breadcrumbs. Add enough chilled water, a little at a time, for it to come together in a soft dough. Knead gently into a ball, wrap in clingfilm and chill for 15 minutes. Meanwhile, heat the oven to 200°C/400°F/gas 6.

2 For the frangipane, cream the butter and sugar in a bowl until light and fluffy. Gradually beat in the eggs and rum, then fold in the flour and ground almonds.

3 Roll out half the chilled pastry on a lightly floured surface to 3mm thick. Stamp out 12 rounds using the fluted cutter, then use to line a bun tin. Repeat with the remaining pastry to line the second tin. Place a teaspoonful of mincemeat in each pastry case.

4 Top each mince pie with a heaped teaspoonful of the frangipane mixture, place in the heated oven and bake for 20–25 minutes until golden. Cool on a wire rack before dusting with icing sugar and serving.

THINKING AHEAD

Freeze the cooked pies in their tins until solid, then transfer to freezer bags and freeze for up to 3 months. Warm through from frozen in a medium–high oven.

PAUL'S MINCEMEAT AND MARZIPAN COURONNE

SERVES 12

250g strong white bread flour, plus extra for dusting
5g salt
8g fast-action dried yeast
50g unsalted butter, softened
135ml full-fat milk
1 medium egg, lightly beaten
oil, for greasing
1 x 400g jar of mincemeat

For the marzipan
90g caster sugar

140g icing sugar, plus extra for dusting
220g ground almonds
finely grated zest of 1 orange
1 medium egg, beaten

To finish
50g apricot jam
100g icing sugar
50g slivered pistachio nuts
25g glacé cherries, roughly chopped

1 Put the flour in a large mixing bowl and add the salt to one side of the bowl and the yeast to the other. Add the butter, milk and egg and turn the mixture round with your fingers. Continue to mix until you've picked up all the flour from the sides of the bowl. Use the mixture to clean the inside of the bowl and keep going until you have a soft dough.

2 Tip the dough onto a lightly floured surface and knead for about 6 minutes. Work through the initial wet stage until the dough starts to form a soft, smooth skin. When the dough feels smooth and silky, put it into a bowl. Cover with clingfilm and leave to rise until at least doubled in size, 30 minutes–1 hour. Line a baking sheet with non-stick baking paper or silicone paper.

3 To make the marzipan, put the caster sugar, icing sugar and ground almonds into a large bowl and mix well. Stir in the orange zest and beaten egg until evenly combined and the mixture

begins to form a paste. Tip onto a work surface lightly dusted with icing sugar and knead until smooth. Wrap in clingfilm and chill for at least 3 hours before use.

4 Turn the risen dough onto a lightly floured surface. Without knocking it back, roll it out into a rectangle, about 33 x 25cm. Turn the dough 90 degrees if necessary, so you have a long edge facing you. Spread the mincemeat evenly over the dough.

5 Roll out the marzipan thinly on a lightly floured surface to a rectangle the same size as the dough and lay it over the mincemeat. Roll up the dough tightly, like a swiss roll, starting from the long side furthest from you. Roll it slightly to seal, then cut it almost in half lengthways, leaving it just joined at one end, like a pair of legs. Twist the 2 dough lengths together, like a rope, then join the ends to form a circular crown, or 'couronne'. Transfer to the lined baking sheet.

6 Put the tray inside a large, clean plastic bag and leave to prove for 30 minutes–1 hour, until the dough springs back quickly if you prod it lightly with your finger. Meanwhile, heat the oven to 220°C/425°F/gas 7.

7 Place the couronne in the heated oven and bake for 25 minutes until risen and golden, then transfer to a wire rack. Gently heat the apricot jam with a splash of water, sieve it, then brush over the warm couronne to glaze. Leave to cool.

8 Mix the icing sugar with 1 tablespoon water to make a thin icing. Brush over the cooled couronne and sprinkle with the pistachios and glacé cherries.

THINKING AHEAD

Make the couronne to the end of the second proving stage in step 6, then freeze until solid and wrap well in baking paper and clingfilm or foil and freeze for up to 3 months. Defrost fully at room temperature before baking and icing.

MINI SPICED APPLE DOUGHNUTS

These delicious little bites are filled with a lovely spiced apple filling,
but you could use cherry or raspberry jam if you prefer a more classic version.

MAKES 12

YOU WILL NEED: A PIPING BAG, FITTED WITH A MEDIUM PLAIN NOZZLE

200g strong white bread flour,
   plus extra for dusting
a pinch of salt
50g cold unsalted butter,
   diced
1 x 7g sachet fast-action dried
   yeast
2 tablespoons caster sugar,
   plus extra to sprinkle
1 medium egg, beaten

80ml lukewarm full-fat milk
sunflower oil, for deep-frying
   and greasing

For the apple filling
2 Bramley apples, peeled,
   cored and chopped into
   small pieces
2 Cox apples, peeled, cored
   and chopped into small pieces

3 tablespoons caster sugar
1 cinnamon stick
4 cloves
½ teaspoon ground ginger
1 vanilla pod, slit in half
   lengthways
a good splash of brandy

1 Put the flour and salt into a large bowl, then rub in the butter with your fingertips until the mixture resembles coarse crumbs. Stir through the yeast and sugar, then make a well in the centre. Mix the egg with the milk and pour into the well. Mix quickly until it comes together into a soft dough.

2 Knead the dough on a lightly floured surface for 5 minutes until smooth and supple. Lightly oil a clean bowl and place the dough in it. Cover with a clean tea towel and leave in a warm place for 1 hour or until doubled in size.

3 Meanwhile, place all the filling ingredients in a pan with a splash of water and cook gently over a low heat, stirring, until the apples are soft. Remove the aromatics and whizz to a purée in a food processor or blender. Set aside to cool.

4 Line a baking sheet with greaseproof paper. Knock back the dough and divide into 12 evenly sized pieces, then roll each into a smooth ball. Place spaced well apart on the baking tray and loosely cover with a sheet of lightly oiled clingfilm. Leave for 45 minutes in a warm place or until doubled in size again.

5 Heat the sunflower oil in a large, deep pan, no more than one-third full, to 170°C (a cube of bread will brown in about 30 seconds). Cook the doughnuts in batches of 2 or 3, frying for 30 seconds–1 minute on each side until golden and cooked through. Remove with a slotted spoon and drain on kitchen paper.

6 While the doughnuts are still warm, spoon the filling into a piping bag fitted with a medium plain nozzle or into a squeezy bottle with a nozzle end.

CONTINUED

Make a little slit in the side of each doughnut with the tip of a small, sharp knife, then squeeze some of the apple purée into the centre. Roll the filled doughnuts gently in caster sugar to coat completely, or dust well using a dredger. Serve warm or allow to cool.

TIP

To make these even more festive, mix caster sugar with ground cinnamon and use this to sprinkle over at the end of cooking.

THINKING AHEAD

Make the doughnuts up to the end of step 4 and freeze in a single layer until solid, then wrap well in baking paper and pack into a freezer container. Defrost fully before frying and filling. The filling can also be frozen, in a small container.

CHRISTMAS FRUIT BREAD

Fruit bread is a great staple to have on hand as it can double up as a lovely breakfast or teatime treat, and is delicious toasted and buttered. It is ideal for sharing, as you can tear the fruity, spiced dough apart with your hands. Pictured overleaf.

MAKES 1 LOAF

100g each of sultanas and raisins
50g each of dried apple and dried apricots, roughly chopped
3 tablespoons Calvados or brandy
500g strong white bread flour, plus extra for dusting

1 x 7g sachet fast-action dried yeast
1 teaspoon salt
1 teaspoon ground allspice
1 teaspoon ground cinnamon
a good grating of fresh nutmeg
175ml warm milk
75g butter, melted
75g caster sugar

2 medium eggs, beaten
30g chopped mixed peel
finely grated zest of ½ orange

To glaze
50g caster sugar
1 tablespoon honey
100ml orange juice

1 Put all the dried fruit in a small pan with the Calvados or brandy and warm gently over a low heat for 1–2 minutes. Remove from the heat and give it a stir, then cover and set aside to soak for at least 1 hour: the longer the better.

2 Mix the flour, yeast, salt and spices in a large bowl and make a well in the centre. Mix the milk, melted butter, sugar and eggs together, pour into the well and mix until it comes together into a soft dough.

3 Turn the dough out onto a lightly floured surface and knead for 5–10 minutes until smooth and elastic. Put the dough in a clean bowl, cover with a clean tea towel and leave to rise in a warm place for 1–2 hours or until doubled in size.

4 Punch down the dough with your knuckles to knock out the air and press it out on a lightly floured surface to a rough rectangle. Sprinkle the soaked fruit, mixed peel and orange zest over the surface, then roll it up. Gently knead to distribute the fruit evenly through the dough.

5 Weigh your dough, cut off about 350g and shape it into a ball. Place in the centre of a lightly floured baking sheet. Divide the rest of the dough into 6 equal-sized pieces, roll into balls and place around the larger ball, not quite touching. Cover with a clean tea towel and leave in a warm place for 1 hour until doubled in size again. Meanwhile, heat the oven to 200°C/400°F/gas 6.

6 Place the risen bread in the heated oven and bake for 20 minutes, then reduce the temperature to 180°C/350°F/gas 4 and bake for a further 40–45 minutes until golden brown and risen, covering it loosely with foil if the top browns too quickly. Turn out onto a wire rack.

7 Melt the sugar and honey in a pan with the orange juice then bubble until you have a light syrup. Brush the glaze all over the warm buns then leave to cool completely.

MARY'S MINCEMEAT STREUSEL

MAKES 16 SLICES
YOU WILL NEED: A 23 X 33CM SWISS ROLL TIN, GREASED

For the mincemeat
100g currants
100g raisins
100g sultanas
100g dried cranberries
100g dried apricots, chopped
50g mixed peel
1 large cooking apple, peeled,
  cored and roughly chopped
75g butter, cubed
25g whole blanched almonds,
  roughly chopped

125g light muscovado sugar
¼ teaspoon ground cinnamon
½ teaspoon ground mixed
  spice
finely grated zest of 1 lemon
  and juice of ½
100ml brandy, rum or sherry

For the topping
75g butter
75g self-raising flour
40g semolina

40g caster sugar
icing sugar, for dusting

For the pastry
175g plain flour, plus extra
  for dusting
1½ tablespoons icing sugar,
  sifted
100g cold unsalted butter,
  cubed
1–2 tablespoons cold water

1 For the mincemeat, place all the ingredients except the alcohol in a large pan and cook over a low heat, stirring occasionally, for about 10 minutes. Remove from the heat, leave to cool, then stir in the brandy, rum or sherry.

2 For the topping, melt the butter and allow to cool slightly. Mix the flour, semolina and caster sugar together in a bowl. Pour over the melted butter and mix until it combines to form a dough. Wrap in clingfilm and chill in the freezer for 30 minutes.

3 For the pastry, put the flour and icing sugar in a mixing bowl and rub in the butter until the mixture resembles coarse breadcrumbs. Add just enough cold water to mix to a firm dough. (If you prefer, use a food processor to make the pastry.) If time allows, wrap the pastry in clingfilm and chill for about 30 minutes. Heat the oven to 200°C/400°F/gas 6.

4 Roll out the pastry on a lightly floured surface to a rectangle slightly larger than the swiss roll tin, then use it to line the base and sides of the greased tin, patching any gaps if necessary. Spread the mincemeat evenly over the pastry base. Trim the pastry level to the top edges of the tin. Using a coarse grater, grate the topping over the mincemeat and spread out evenly. Place in the heated oven and bake for about 25–30 minutes until golden brown.

5 Remove from the oven and leave to cool to warm, then cut into 16 slices, dust with icing sugar and serve still warm, with cream or brandy butter.

THINKING AHEAD

Freeze the cooked slices in a plastic container for up to 3 months. Thaw at room temperature in the container for 4 hours or overnight, and reheat in a medium oven for about 20 minutes.

APPLE AND PEAR CRUMBLE SLICES

This is a great pudding for families – somewhere between a crumble and a cake – that should be served warm with cream, custard or ice cream.

MAKES 8
YOU WILL NEED: A 20CM SQUARE CAKE TIN, LIGHTLY BUTTERED

For the filling
40g unsalted butter
4 Cox apples, peeled, cored and cut into wedges
2 pears such as Comice or Concorde, peeled, cored and cut into cubes
3 tablespoons caster sugar
1 vanilla pod, slit lengthways and seeds scraped

For the crumble
400g plain flour
2 teaspoons ground ginger
85g caster sugar
a good pinch of salt
200g cold unsalted butter, cut into pieces
finely grated zest of 1 lemon
2 medium egg yolks
95ml soured cream

1 Heat the oven to 180°C/350°C/gas 4. For the filling, melt the butter in a non-stick pan and add the apples, pears, sugar and vanilla seeds. Cook gently for a couple of minutes until starting to soften but not broken down. Set aside to cool.

2 Mix the flour with the ginger, sugar and salt. Rub in the butter with your fingertips until the mixture resembles coarse crumbs. Add the lemon zest, egg yolks and soured cream, but don't over mix; it should just be coming together but still crumbly.

3 Spoon two-thirds of the crumble mixture into the prepared tin and press it down lightly with your fingers into an even layer. Don't press it too hard. Spoon the cooled fruit and any juice on top and then scatter with the remaining topping.

4 Place in the heated oven and bake for 30–35 minutes until golden. Allow to cool in the tin for at least 15 minutes before turning out to serve with cream, custard or vanilla ice cream.

TIP

Don't waste your vanilla pod. Keep a bottle of vodka in the freezer and every time you use a vanilla pod, pop it into the bottle. Over time it will become thick, dark and rich, and is amazing for flavouring sauces, as well as for cocktails. You can also place it in a jar of caster or granulated sugar, so it infuses the sugar with its flavour.

THINKING AHEAD

Freeze the finished, cooled crumble in its tin, wrapped well. Warm through from frozen, covered loosely with foil, in a medium oven.

EDD'S SPICED CHOCOLATE BUNDT CAKE

Everyone's busy at Christmas – but nobody wants to be stressed! One of the best ways to enjoy it calmly is to prepare ahead, and having this beautiful spiced chocolate cake waiting in your freezer is the perfect solution. Everyone will want a slice, or two!

THE GREAT
BRITISH BAKE OFF
**EDD
KIMBER**
2010

MAKES 1 LARGE CAKE
YOU WILL NEED: A 25CM DIAMETER, 2 LITRE BUNDT TIN

200g unsalted butter, diced, plus extra for greasing
30g cocoa powder
100ml hot water
200g dark chocolate (60–70% cocoa solids), roughly chopped

300g light muscovado sugar
4 large eggs
175g self-raising flour
1 teaspoon baking powder
3 teaspoons ground ginger
2 teaspoons ground mixed spice

1½ teaspoons ground cinnamon
40g chopped glacé or crystallised ginger

For the glaze
300ml double cream
160g dark chocolate (60–70% cocoa solids), finely chopped

1 Heat the oven to 180°C/350°F/gas 4 and grease the bundt tin well, making sure to get into all of the crevices, or the cake may stick to the tin.

2 Put the cocoa into a small bowl and pour over the hot water, whisking together until smooth. Put the butter and chocolate in a heatproof bowl set over a pan of simmering water, and melt, stirring occasionally. Remove from the heat and allow to cool slightly.

3 Put the sugar and eggs in a large bowl and, using an electric mixer, whisk until thick and pale. With the mixer still running, pour in the chocolate and mix until smooth and fully combined.

4 Whisk together the flour, baking powder and spices in a separate bowl. Sift the dry ingredients over the chocolate mixture and fold together until no lumps remain. Add the ginger and the cocoa mixture and mix to combine. Pour into the prepared tin, then place on a baking sheet, transfer to the heated oven and bake for

40–45 minutes or until a skewer inserted into the thickest part of the cake comes out clean. Leave to cool in the tin for about 10 minutes before carefully inverting onto a wire rack set over a parchment-lined baking tray to cool completely.

5 To make the glaze, put the cream and chocolate into a medium saucepan and place over a low-medium heat, stirring regularly until the chocolate has melted and you have a smooth mixture. Set aside to cool for a few minutes.

6 Pour the glaze over the cooled cake, trying to cover the entire surface. Allow the glaze to set before carefully transferring to a plate to serve.

THINKING AHEAD

You can freeze the cake at the end of step 4, before glazing it, on a baking sheet until solid, then wrap well in baking paper and clingfilm or foil and freeze for up to 3 months. Defrost fully before glazing.

COME ON OVER

CHRISTMAS EVE AND CHRISTMAS DAY

CHRISTMAS EVE AND CHRISTMAS DAY

The big day is finally here! This chapter is packed full of festive bakes, both new and old, for the main event.

Christmas Eve and Christmas Day are rich with culinary traditions: those that are part of our wider culture, and the equally important little rituals we have created ourselves with our own families.

For many, the big day revolves around a roast turkey, but if you want something a little different this year, a Baked Christmas Ham (page 136) makes a great alternative. The dish harks back to the boar's head traditionally served in Scandinavian countries on St Stephens Day – and of course, leaves plenty of cold cuts for Boxing Day.

In much of Europe, the big day is not the 25th December but Christmas Eve, when presents are exchanged and the celebratory dinner is served, often of carp or other fish. For many of us it wouldn't be Christmas without generous helpings of smoked salmon and it is the Scandinavians we have to thank for this tradition, too. What could be more delicious than a glass of champagne with a warm Potato Blini and Smoked Salmon (page 135) or a creamy Smoked Salmon Soufflé Omelette (page 132)?

The Yule log, a large log decorated in holly and evergreen, kept alight for the 12 days of Christmas to bring luck to the household, was an ancient pagan custom that has been transformed over centuries into the delicious chocolate log that children love (page 149). And Christmas pudding, which began in medieval times as a thick kind of porridge called frumenty, full of dried fruits and spices, has become a staple of the Christmas table. The recipe on page 145 is made without any suet which can make a pud heavy and dense.

These are the days to kick back after all the festive preparations and eat, drink and be merry.

CHRISTMAS EVE VENISON PIE

Venison is a fabulous seasonal meat that can take some really punchy flavours in a pie. If you can't get your hands on some good-sized chunks of venison, try using shin of beef instead. Pictured overleaf.

SERVES 6–8
YOU WILL NEED: A 1.8 LITRE PIE DISH; A PIE FUNNEL

1.5kg venison haunch or shoulder, cut into large chunks

3 tablespoons plain flour, seasoned with salt and pepper

6–8 tablespoons olive oil

2 large red onions, finely sliced

4 garlic cloves, flattened with the back of a knife

2 celery sticks, chopped

1 large carrot, finely chopped

150g Portobello or flat mushrooms, sliced

a few sprigs each of fresh rosemary and thyme

2 fresh bay leaves

5 juniper berries, lightly crushed

250ml dry white wine

250ml good quality chicken stock

1 small egg, beaten with 1 tablespoon milk

salt and black pepper

For the pastry

175g plain flour, plus extra for dusting

25g wholemeal flour

a good pinch of salt

100g cold unsalted butter, cut into cubes

1 medium egg yolk

2 tablespoons full-fat cream cheese mixed with 1 tablespoon water

1 Heat the oven to 170°C/325°F/gas 3. Dust the venison pieces in the seasoned flour. Heat a couple of tablespoons of the oil in a large non-stick frying pan and brown the meat in batches, adding more oil if necessary. Once browned, spoon the pieces into a large flameproof casserole.

2 Heat a little more oil in the pan and gently fry the onion for 5 minutes, then add the garlic, celery and carrot. Fry for a further 10 minutes then add to the casserole. Heat the remaining oil and fry the mushrooms until golden brown, then spoon into the casserole and add the herbs and juniper.

3 Set the pot over a high heat and add the wine, season well and allow to bubble for a couple of minutes until it has reduced by half, before pouring over the stock. Once simmering, cover with a lid, transfer to the heated oven and cook for 2½–3 hours until the meat is really tender and falling apart, removing the lid for the last 30 minutes of cooking. Allow to cool.

4 To make the pastry, mix the flours and salt then rub in the butter with your fingertips until it resembles breadcrumbs. Add the egg and cream cheese mixture and mix quickly with a flat-bladed knife. Once it starts to come together,

use your hands to bring it into a ball and knead it briefly until smooth. Shape into a disc, wrap in clingfilm and chill for 10 minutes. Heat the oven to 200°C/400°F/gas 6.

5 Spoon the cold pie filling into a 1.8 litre pie dish and place a pie funnel in the centre of the pie. Roll out the pastry on a lightly floured surface. Brush the edge of the pie dish with the beaten egg mixture and top with the pastry. Make little decorations out of the leftover pastry trimmings and attach them to the pie top with the egg glaze. Brush all over with the egg glaze, place in the heated oven and bake for 35–40 minutes until golden and bubbling.

THINKING AHEAD

You can chill the filling overnight to finish the pie the next day, or freeze it for up to 3 months.

JOHN'S PEANUT BUTTER, POPCORN AND CHOCOLATE FUDGE TORTE

THE GREAT BRITISH BAKE OFF

JOHN WHAITE

2012

Christmas is undoubtedly a time of indulgence, or rather overindulgence. This torte is not only a feast for the stomach with its layers of soft cake, sweet mousse and decadent fudge, but because of those defined layers, also a feast for the eyes; perfect for a Christmas Eve treat.

SERVES 12–16
YOU WILL NEED: A 23CM ROUND SPRINGFORM CAKE TIN, BASE ONLY GREASED AND LINED

For the genoise cake

5 large eggs

140g caster sugar

120g plain flour

40g cocoa powder

50g butter, melted and cooled

For the peanut butter and popcorn filling

75g toffee popcorn

200ml double cream

90g sweetened, smooth peanut butter

50g condensed milk

100g mascarpone cheese

For the chocolate fudge topping

250g condensed milk

50g smooth, sweetened peanut butter

50ml double cream

200g dark chocolate, around 35–40% cocoa solids, broken into pieces

For the caramelised popcorn and to finish

100g caster sugar

50g toffee popcorn

cocoa powder, for dusting

1 Heat the oven to 200°C/400°F/gas 6. Put the eggs into the bowl of an electric mixer fitted with whisk attachment and beat gently for 1 minute. Add the sugar and turn the mixer up to full speed. Whisk for about 5 minutes, until the mixture has about quadrupled in volume and the ribbon stage is achieved: when you lift out the whisk and draw a figure-of-eight with the falling mixture, it should sit proud on the surface for 3 or more seconds.

2 Sift over the flour and cocoa powder and very gently fold in, along with the melted butter. Pour into the prepared tin, transfer to the heated oven and bake for 25 minutes, or until risen and a skewer inserted into the centre comes out clean. Invert the tin onto a wire rack and leave the cake to cool completely, still in its tin.

3 For the filling, blitz the popcorn in a food processor to a sandy rubble. Add the cream and blitz until the cream just thickens – this shouldn't take more than 10 seconds. Add the peanut butter, condensed milk and mascarpone and blitz again until the mixture is thick and spreadable. Scoop into a bowl and chill until needed.

4 Slice the cooled cake in half as neatly as possible (see Tip, overleaf). Remove the baking paper and clean the cake tin, then place one half

CONTINUED

of the cake back in the tin, pressing it down gently so that it fills the bottom. Pile the peanut butter and popcorn filling on top and spread it out evenly with a small palette knife or the back of a spoon. Top with the second half of cake and chill in the fridge.

5 Meanwhile, to make the fudge topping, put all the ingredients into a medium saucepan and set over a very low heat. Stirring quite often, allow the ingredients to slowly melt together into a smooth, glossy fudge. Pour this over the cake, still in the tin, and allow to set in the fridge for at least 1 hour.

6 To make the caramelised popcorn, place a sheet of baking paper on the work surface. Heat a medium pan over a medium-high heat. Add the sugar and slowly let it melt, stirring every so often, for about 8 minutes, until it turns a fairly dark caramel. Immediately add the popcorn and stir to coat well, then tip onto the baking paper and allow to cool completely.

7 Remove the cake from the fridge a good hour before serving. Run a knife around the edge and release it from the tin. Transfer to a serving plate, sift cocoa powder over the top, and festively embellish with the caramelised popcorn pieces.

TIP

To cut a cake neatly in half (see step 4), cut a groove round the middle of the cake, using a breadknife, then insert a piece of cotton thread all around the groove and pull it through.

THINKING AHEAD

To prepare this in advance, freeze the filled cake wrapped in plenty of clingfilm. Defrost in the fridge the night before serving, then add the topping and finish.

RUDOLF'S CARROT CAKE

Father Christmas and Rudolf will be over the moon when they receive a little slice of this moist carrot cake before heading back to the North Pole. It is best eaten on the day it is iced, as the icing needs to be kept in the fridge, which can make the sponge a little heavy. Pictured overleaf.

SERVES 12–14
YOU WILL NEED: 2 X 20CM LOOSE-BOTTOMED SANDWICH TINS, BUTTERED AND LINED

4 medium eggs
225ml sunflower oil
175g light muscovado sugar
3 tablespoons maple syrup
2 teaspoons ground cinnamon
300g self-raising flour
1 teaspoon baking powder

½ teaspoon bicarbonate
    of soda
50g pine nuts, toasted
350g (2–3) carrots, coarsely
    grated

For the icing and decorating
400g full-fat cream cheese

50ml double cream
75g icing sugar
chocolate icing
chocolate sprinkles
red icing
red sugar sprinkles

1 Heat the oven to 180°C/350°F/gas 4. Put the eggs, oil, sugar and maple syrup in a bowl and whisk with a hand-held electric whisk for 4–5 minutes until the mixture becomes creamy.

2 Sift together the cinnamon, flour, baking powder and bicarbonate of soda, then fold gradually into the mixture. Gently fold in the pine nuts and carrots.

3 Divide the mixture evenly between the prepared tins, place in the heated oven and bake for 35–40 minutes or until a skewer inserted into the centre comes out clean. Leave to cool in the tins for 10 minutes, then turn out onto a wire rack to cool completely.

4 For the icing, beat the cream cheese and double cream together until smooth, then beat in the icing sugar until the mixture is smooth and creamy.

5 To assemble, place one of the sponges top-down on a plate and spread the surface generously with one-third of the icing. Top with the other cake and cover the top with the remaining icing. Smooth the top of the

icing flat with a palette knife before decorating. Use a cocktail stick to mark out where you want your design to go. Mark the antlers, eyes and outline of the nose (see overleaf). Use chocolate icing to pipe the eyes and the antlers, then scatter with chocolate sprinkles. Use red icing to pipe the outline of the nose and fill with red sugar sprinkles. Serve immediately.

TIP

You can buy ready-made coloured icing in tubes with piping nozzles, which are really handy for cake decorating. If you can't find them, make up a buttercream icing by beating equal quantities of butter and icing sugar together, then adding food colouring for red or a couple of tablespoons of cocoa for chocolate. You can then put these into piping bags fitted with a small plain nozzle to decorate your cakes.

BRIOCHE SNOWMEN

Little pillows of enriched buttery brioche, served warm with jam or maple syrup, are a perfect morning treat. You need to chill the dough overnight, so start this recipe the day before you need it.

MAKES 12
YOU WILL NEED: A 12-HOLE, ROUND-BOTTOMED BUN TRAY

25g fresh yeast OR 2 x 7g sachets fast-action dried yeast
125ml lukewarm water
4 tablespoons caster sugar

570g plain flour, plus extra for dusting
2 teaspoons salt
4 medium eggs and 1 medium yolk, to glaze

125ml lukewarm milk
125g unsalted butter, diced and softened, plus extra, melted, for greasing

1 Cream the fresh yeast with the water, or sprinkle the dried yeast over the surface of the water and stand for 5 minutes until lightly frothy.

2 Mix the sugar, flour and salt in a large bowl and make a well in the centre. Beat the whole eggs into the warm milk, then pour into the well in the flour and add the yeast and water mixture. Mix well to form a soft dough.

3 Add half the diced butter to the dough and beat with a wooden spoon until smooth. At this point the dough is really soft. Dot the remaining butter all over the surface of the dough, cover with a clean tea towel and leave in a warm place to double in size, 1–2 hours depending on how warm your kitchen is.

4 Punch the risen dough down with your hands and then beat vigorously with your hands for 5 minutes. You want to make the dough really elastic, so you need to pull and stretch it up and out of the bowl then back down. When you can stretch it up to the height of your shoulder without it breaking, you have done enough beating.

5 Cover the bowl with lightly greased clingfilm, place in the fridge and chill overnight (this will make it easier to work).

6 The next day, brush the bun tray with melted butter. Turn the dough out onto a lightly floured surface and knead briefly until smooth. Weigh the dough, cut off a quarter and set aside. Divide the larger piece into 12, roll each into a ball and place in the buttered moulds. Roll the remaining dough into 12 small balls.

7 Using scissors, cut a cross in the top of each of the larger dough balls in the moulds, then place a smaller ball on top (to form the heads of the snowmen). Cover the bun tray with a clean tea towel and leave to rise for 30 minutes–1 hour until doubled in size. Meanwhile, heat the oven to 200°C/400°F/gas 6.

8 Beat the extra egg yolk with a little water and use to brush the tops of the risen brioche. Place in the heated oven and bake for 20 minutes until firm, well risen and lovely and golden. Turn out onto a wire rack to cool a little before serving.

TIP

Plain flour is traditional for a classic French brioche, but if you prefer yours a little more robust and bready you can use strong bread flour or experiment mixing the two together.

SMOKED SALMON SOUFFLÉ OMELETTE

Eggs and smoked salmon make an indulgent and glorious breakfast combination. Rather than having to make individual omelettes for everyone, this recipe makes life easy by serving the whole table from one pan.

~~~~~~~~~~~~~~~~~~~~~~~~~~~~~~~~~~~~

SERVES 4–6
YOU WILL NEED: A 25CM OVENPROOF FRYING PAN

60g butter
30g plain flour
200ml full-fat milk
100ml double cream
6 large eggs, separated
200g sustainable smoked
   salmon, finely sliced

a small bunch of fresh chives,
   snipped
75ml crème fraîche
15g Parmesan cheese, grated
salt and black pepper

~~~~~~~~~~~~~~~~~~~~~~~~~~~~~~~~~~~~

1 Heat the grill to high. Melt 30g of the butter in a small pan over a medium heat, then add the flour and stir for 1 minute. Gradually add the milk and cream, stirring, until it is a thick sauce. Season and remove from the heat.

2 Spoon into a bowl and stir in the egg yolks, salmon, chives, crème fraîche and Parmesan. Whisk the egg whites in a separate bowl until they form soft peaks, then gently fold them into the egg yolk mixture.

3 Melt the remaining butter in a 25cm ovenproof frying pan over a medium heat. Once foaming, pour in the omelette mixture. Turn the heat down to low and cook for 2–3 minutes until just set on the bottom. Do not stir.

4 Pop the frying pan under the heated grill for 4–5 minutes until it has puffed up and is a golden brown on the top. Cut into slices and serve immediately, with buttered sourdough toast.

POTATO BLINIS WITH SMOKED SALMON

Not strictly speaking blinis, these little potato pancakes are just right for a canapé, served with a glass of cold fizz.

MAKES 26

250g floury potatoes, peeled and chopped
50ml milk
60g self-raising flour
2 large eggs, separated
50ml soured cream
1 tablespoon creamed horseradish

vegetable oil, for frying
200g sustainable smoked salmon, sliced
lemon wedges, to serve
salt and black pepper

For the herb crème fraîche
200ml crème fraîche

3 tablespoons finely chopped fresh dill
2 tablespoons finely chopped fresh chives
a good squeeze of lemon juice

1 Put the potatoes in a pan of cold salted water, bring to the boil and simmer for 12–15 minutes until tender. Drain and put through a ricer (or mash with a masher) and mix with the milk. Transfer to a bowl to cool.

2 Once cold, beat in the flour, egg yolks, soured cream and horseradish. Season well. Whisk the egg whites in a clean bowl until they form stiff peaks. Mix a spoonful of the whites into the potato mixture to loosen it, then fold in the rest of the whites.

3 Heat a tiny amount of oil in a heavy-based frying pan (it may be easier to wipe the pan with kitchen paper dipped in oil). Dollop tablespoons of the mixture into the hot pan and flatten slightly. Cook over a medium heat for 1 minute, then turn them over and fry for a further 30 seconds until golden on both sides. Keep warm as you cook the remaining blinis, lightly oiling the pan between batches.

4 Mix the crème fraîche with the herbs and lemon juice and season well. Serve the blinis just warm with a dollop of the herb crème fraîche and some smoked salmon on top, and lemon wedges on the side.

TIP

A ricer is really useful for this as it gets the mash really lovely and smooth. If you don't have a ricer you can mash with a regular potato masher or better still, push the mash through a metal sieve. This may see a little laborious but it's worth it for the light and fluffy result.

THINKING AHEAD

The blinis will freeze well. Leave to cool completely, then freeze between layers of greaseproof paper in a sealed container. Defrost in a single layer before warming gently in a low oven.

BAKED CHRISTMAS HAM

A real centrepiece, a whole ham is a thing of beauty. It is worth getting a whole one even if you don't have a very large crowd to feed, as the leftovers will keep you going long after the day itself. If you want, just ask your butcher for a smaller chunk of the gammon on the bone. You need to start this recipe at least the day before you want to eat it.

~~~~~~~~~~~~~~~~

SERVES 10, WITH LEFTOVERS
YOU WILL NEED: A DEEP ROASTING TIN (WITH A RACK) BIG ENOUGH TO HOLD THE HAM

1 large onion, quartered

2 carrots, roughly chopped

3 bay leaves

a handful of fresh parsley stalks

a handful of fresh thyme sprigs

8 black peppercorns

6 allspice berries, lightly crushed

1.5 litres medium dry cider

9–10kg whole unsmoked ham on the bone, soaked for 8 hours in cold water, changing the water regularly

3 tablespoons golden syrup

2 tablespoons black treacle

2 teaspoons ground ginger

a good pinch of English mustard powder

juice of ½ orange

2–3 tablespoons demerara sugar

~~~~~~~~~~~~~~~~

1 Heat the oven to 120°C/250°F/gas ½. Put the onion, carrots, bay leaves, herbs, peppercorns and allspice in the roasting tin. Pour the cider over, then put the rack on top.

2 Sit the soaked and drained ham on the rack and cover with a large tent of foil, sealing it well. Put on the hob over a high heat and bring to the boil. Simmer for 15 minutes, then transfer to the warm oven and bake for 8 hours or overnight.

3 Remove from the oven and increase the temperature to 180°C/350°F/gas 4. Using a sharp knife, carefully peel the skin away from the ham, leaving behind as much of the fat as you can.

4 Mix the syrup and treacle with the ginger, mustard powder and orange juice and smear all over the ham. Sprinkle with the sugar, place in the heated oven and bake for 45 minutes–1 hour until sticky and piping hot throughout.

THINKING AHEAD

You can bake the ham and leave it in a cool place (such as a cellar, unheated porch or secure garage, if the weather is nice and cold) for up to 24 hours before you want to finish it in the hot oven. Leave the skin on and make sure it is wrapped well in foil.

ULTIMATE POTATO GRATIN

A bold statement but a true one: this is the ultimate in potato gratins. Rich and cheesy, it really is one to keep out the winter blues. The best bit, though, is its lack of prep, as the potatoes go in raw and gently cook in all the lovely creamy sauce. Pictured on the previous page.

SERVES 8–10
YOU WILL NEED: A 30 X 24CM X 5.5CM OVENPROOF DISH OR ROASTING TIN

25g unsalted butter

1 tablespoon olive oil

2 onions, finely chopped

2–3 sprigs of fresh oregano, leaves stripped

4 garlic cloves, crushed

2.2kg floury potatoes, peeled

2 tablespoons plain flour

75g Cheddar cheese, grated

75g Gruyère cheese, grated

a handful of fresh flat-leaf parsley, leaves roughly chopped

400ml double cream

200ml full-fat milk

salt and black pepper

1 Heat the oven to 170°C/325°F/gas 3. Heat the butter and oil in a frying pan, add the onion and fry over a low heat for 10 minutes until soft and golden. Add the oregano and garlic and fry for 1 further minute. Set aside to cool a little.

2 Slice the potatoes into 5–6mm rounds and mix with the onion mixture, flour, all but a handful of each cheese, and the parsley. Season well, then layer up in an ovenproof dish or roasting tin. Mix the cream and milk together and season. Pour over the potatoes and scatter over the remaining cheeses.

3 Place in the heated oven and bake for 1 hour 45 minutes until bubbling and golden, and the potatoes are cooked. If it browns too quickly, cover the dish loosely with foil and continue to cook. Allow to stand for 10 minutes before serving.

WATERCRESS AND GRUYÈRE SOUFFLÉS

Don't be afraid of soufflés – they may seem high pressure, but actually are surprisingly forgiving. It is even possible to take one out of the oven, dig your spoon into it and then pop it back if it is still not done. Ideally you want to end up with about a spoonful of slightly gooey filling in the middle and a lovely golden crust.

MAKES 8
YOU WILL NEED: 8 X 200ML RAMEKIN DISHES

75g butter, plus extra, melted, for greasing
a handful of fresh fine white breadcrumbs
200g watercress
a little splash of boiling water
60g plain flour
450ml milk
a good pinch of cayenne pepper
a grating of fresh nutmeg
6 large eggs, separated
150g Gruyère cheese, grated
50g Parmesan cheese, grated
salt and black pepper

1 Heat the oven to 200°C/400°C/gas 6 with a baking sheet inside to heat up. Brush the inside of each ramekin with melted butter and sprinkle with breadcrumbs.

2 Wilt the watercress in a pan with the splash of boiling water. Rinse to cool under cold water, then squeeze out as much water as possible and very finely chop.

3 Melt the butter in a pan, stir in the flour and cook for 2 minutes. Gradually add the milk, stirring, and bring to the boil. Boil for 2 minutes, until very thick. Remove from the heat and stir in the cayenne, nutmeg and egg yolks. Season well. Stir in the watercress and cheeses. Whisk the egg whites in a clean bowl until they form stiff peaks. Mix a spoonful into the mixture to loosen, before gently folding in the rest, being careful not to knock the air out.

4 Divide the mixture between the ramekins, almost up to the rim (if you have been excellent at folding you may have a little mixture left over). Run a finger around the edge. Place on the heated baking sheet and bake for 12–14 minutes. Don't open the oven door until three-quarters of the way through the cooking time or your soufflés may deflate. The soufflés should be well risen but with the slightest wobble in the centre. Serve immediately with a salad.

TIP

These make not only an ideal starter, but a very good main course for vegetarians. In this case, use 4 x 300ml ramekins, filling them to the top, and bake for a little longer.

BEEF WELLINGTON

A beautifully cooked Beef Wellington, pink and tender in the centre with a crisp golden crust, makes an impressive alternative to the traditional turkey for those wanting something a little different.

SERVES 6

oil, for frying
1–1.2kg aged beef fillet, from the thick end
70g butter
2 small shallots, very finely chopped
2 garlic cloves, very finely chopped
300g Portobello mushrooms, finely chopped
a small bunch of fresh tarragon, finely chopped

2 x 375g blocks of all-butter puff pastry, thawed if frozen
plain flour, for dusting
1 medium egg, beaten

For the parfait
200g chicken livers
1 tablespoon vegetable oil
50ml brandy
75g unsalted butter
a pinch of ground mace or a grating of nutmeg
salt and black pepper

1 To make the parfait, season the chicken livers with salt and pepper. Heat the oil in a pan over a high heat and sear the livers for 1–2 minutes on each side until browned and just cooked. Take off the heat, add the brandy, return to the heat and allow it to bubble away for 1 minute, then transfer to a food processor.

2 Melt the butter until just about to boil. Blitz the livers until smooth then, with the motor running, pour in the hot, melted butter. Add the mace or nutmeg and a little more salt and pepper. Scoop into a bowl, cover and chill in the fridge.

3 Heat a little oil in a heavy-based pan over a high heat, season the beef well and fry until browned all over. Set aside to cool.

4 Melt the butter in a pan over a medium heat, add the shallots and cook for 10 minutes until pale golden. Add the garlic and fry for 1 further minute. Stir in the mushrooms, season well, increase the heat a little and cook for 15–20 minutes until softened and the moisture from the mushrooms has evaporated. Add the tarragon, tip into a bowl and allow to cool completely.

5 Heat the oven to 200°C/400°F/gas 6 with a baking sheet inside to heat up. Roll out one of the blocks of pastry on a lightly floured surface to a rectangle about 25 x 30cm and the thickness of a £1 coin. Place on a (cold) baking sheet lined with non-stick baking paper. Brush the edges of the pastry with the beaten egg and place the seared beef in the centre.

6 Spread the parfait all over the top and sides of the beef, then press the mushroom mixture onto it. Roll out the second block of pastry so that it is 4cm wider and longer than the first. Drape over

CONTINUED

the top of the beef and press the edges together all around, making sure it is pressed snugly around the beef with no air pockets. Trim the edges with a sharp knife and crimp them with your fingertips to seal. Brush all over with the beaten egg. If you have any pastry trimmings, you can decorate the top with little pastry shapes.

7 Lift the Wellington, still on its baking paper, and transfer to the hot baking sheet in the oven. Bake for 30 minutes until golden all over, turning it around after 20 minutes to cook evenly, then set aside to rest for 10 minutes before serving.

TIP

You may find this is a little too much parfait to coat your beef fillet but as it's such delicious stuff it's worth making a bit extra to have in the fridge. You can use as a standby canapé to spread on little toasts with a dollop of cranberry or redcurrant jelly.

MARY'S CHRISTMAS PUDDING

SERVES 6–8

YOU WILL NEED: A 1.4 LITRE PUDDING BASIN, LIGHTLY BUTTERED

450g dried fruit, a mixture
  of sultanas, raisins and
  chopped apricots
1 small cooking apple, peeled,
  cored and roughly chopped
  (about 175g)
finely grated zest and juice of
  1 orange

50ml brandy or rum, plus
  extra for flaming
75g butter, softened
100g light muscovado sugar
2 medium eggs
100g self-raising flour
1 level teaspoon mixed spice
40g fresh white breadcrumbs

40g almonds, roughly
  chopped

For the brandy butter
100g unsalted butter,
  softened
225g icing sugar, sifted
3–5 tablespoons brandy
  or cognac

1 Cut a small square of foil and press it into the base of the buttered basin.

2 Put the dried fruit and apple into a bowl with the orange juice. Add the brandy or rum and leave to marinate for about 1 hour.

3 Put the butter, sugar and orange zest into a large bowl and cream together with a wooden spoon or an electric hand-held whisk until light and fluffy. Gradually beat in the eggs, adding a little flour if the mixture starts to curdle.

4 Sift together the flour and mixed spice, then fold into the creamed mixture with the breadcrumbs and the nuts. Add the dried fruits, apple and their soaking liquid and stir well.

5 Spoon into the prepared pudding basin, pressing the mixture down, and level the top with the back of a spoon. Cover the pudding with a layer of baking parchment and foil, both pleated across the middle to allow for expansion. Tie securely with string and trim off excess paper and foil with scissors.

6 To steam, put the pudding in the top of a steamer filled with simmering water, cover and steam for about 8 hours, topping up the water as necessary. To boil the pudding, put a metal jam jar lid or metal pan lid into the base of a large pan to act as a trivet. Put the pudding on this and pour in enough boiling water to come one-third of the way up the bowl. Cover, bring the water back to the boil, then simmer for about 7 hours, until the pudding is a glorious deep brown colour, topping up the water as necessary.

7 Meanwhile, to make the brandy butter, beat the butter well in a bowl with a wooden spoon until soft (or use an electric hand-held whisk). Beat in the sifted icing sugar until smooth, then add brandy or cognac to taste. Spoon into a serving dish, cover and keep in the fridge.

8 Remove the cooked pudding from the steamer or pan and cool completely. Discard the paper and foil and replace with fresh. Store in a cool, dry place.

9 To serve, steam or boil the pudding for about 1 hour to reheat. Turn the pudding onto a serving plate. To flame, warm 3–4 tablespoons brandy or rum in a small pan, pour it over the hot pudding and set light to it. Serve with the brandy butter.

Pictured overleaf

MARY'S YULE LOG

SERVES 8–10
YOU WILL NEED: A 33 X 23CM SWISS ROLL TIN, LIGHTLY GREASED AND LINED WITH BAKING PARCHMENT (PUSHED RIGHT INTO THE CORNERS); A PIPING BAG FITTED WITH A STAR NOZZLE

4 large eggs
100g caster sugar
65g self-raising flour
40g cocoa powder
icing sugar, for dusting
300ml double cream,
   whipped

For the chocolate ganache topping
300ml double cream
300g dark chocolate, around
   35–40% cocoa solids, broken
   into small pieces

1 Heat the oven to 200°C/400°F/gas 6. Whisk the eggs and sugar in a large bowl, using a hand-held electric whisk, until pale, light and frothy. Sift in the flour and cocoa powder and carefully cut and fold together, using a spatula, until both are incorporated into the egg mixture, taking care not to beat any of the air out of the mixture.

2 Pour into the prepared tin and spread evenly out into the corners. Place in the middle of the heated oven and bake for 8–10 minutes, or until well risen and firm to the touch, and the sides are shrinking away from the edge of the tin.

3 Place a piece of baking parchment bigger than the tin on the work surface. Generously dust with icing sugar, carefully invert the cake onto the paper and remove the bottom lining paper.

4 Score a line with a knife 2.5cm in from one of the longer edges. Starting with this edge, tightly roll up the sponge, rolling up the paper inside as you go. Sit the roll on top of its outside edge to cool completely.

5 Meanwhile, to make the ganache, heat the cream in a pan, to the temperature where you can just keep your finger in it. Remove from the heat and add the chocolate, stirring until melted. Cool to room temperature, then chill in the fridge to firm up (it needs to be very thick for piping).

6 Unfurl the cold swiss roll and remove the paper. Spread the whipped cream over the surface and re-roll tightly. Cut a quarter of the cake off from one end, on the diagonal. Transfer the large piece of cake to a serving plate or board and angle the cut end out from the middle of the large cake, to make a branch.

7 Put the ganache into a piping bag fitted with a star nozzle. Pipe long, thick lines along the cake, covering the cake completely to resemble the bark of a tree. Cover each end with icing or leave un-iced if you prefer to see the cream. Alternatively, just use a palette knife to spread on the icing and create rough bark texture with a fork. Dust with icing sugar and serve.

SALTED CARAMEL AND CHOCOLATE CREAM PROFITEROLES

Profiteroles are glamorously delicious but actually very simple to make, and this is a great dessert to serve when you don't want to have to faff about in the kitchen between courses – you can have all the elements ready in advance so it is just a matter of assembling them before you take it to the table.

~~~~~~

MAKES 20–24
YOU WILL NEED: A PIPING BAG FITTED WITH A MEDIUM PLAIN NOZZLE

75g plain flour

1 teaspoon caster sugar

a pinch of salt

60g unsalted butter, cut into cubes, plus extra for greasing

2 large eggs, beaten

For the chocolate cream filling

100g dark chocolate

400ml double cream (not fridge-cold)

2 tablespoons icing sugar

1 teaspoon vanilla extract

For the salted caramel sauce

200g caster sugar

50g unsalted butter, cut into cubes

60ml double cream

¼ teaspoon fine sea salt

~~~~~~

1 Heat the oven to 200°C/400°F/gas 6. Sift the flour, sugar and salt into a heap on a sheet of baking paper.

2 Put 150ml water and the butter in a pan and heat over a medium heat until the butter melts. Increase the heat and bring to a vigorous rolling boil.

3 Using the baking paper as a funnel, quickly tip the flour mixture into the water and butter, then remove from the heat and beat vigorously with a wooden spoon until the mixture forms a thick paste that comes away cleanly from the sides of the pan.

4 Gradually add the beaten egg, beating between each addition, until you have a smooth, glossy mixture. You may not need all the egg – add just enough to give a thick dropping consistency.

5 Lightly grease a baking sheet. Use 2 teaspoons to dollop walnut-sized balls of the mixture onto the baking sheet, leaving space to allow them to rise. Place on the top shelf of the oven and bake for 15–18 minutes until risen, golden and crisp. Pierce the bottom of each bun with a sharp knife so the steam can escape, then return to the oven for a further 3–4 minutes. Set aside to cool completely on a wire rack.

CONTINUED

PAUL'S KRANSEKAKE

MAKES 1 LARGE KRANSEKAKE
YOU WILL NEED: A SET OF KRANSEKAKE MOULDS; 2 PIPING BAGS,
EACH FITTED WITH A SMALL, PLAIN NOZZLE

500g ground almonds
500g icing sugar, sifted
4 egg whites, beaten
1 teaspoon almond extract
oil, for greasing
semolina, for dusting

For the icing and to decorate
3 egg whites
600g icing sugar, sifted
red food colouring paste
edible glitter

1 To make the dough, tip the ground almonds and icing sugar into a bowl, add the beaten egg whites and the almond extract and mix to a dough with your hands. Cover the bowl with clingfilm and chill for a minimum of 2 hours, preferably overnight.

2 Heat the oven to 200°C/400°F/gas 6. Lightly oil the kransekake moulds and sprinkle with semolina, shaking off any excess. Divide the chilled dough into 6 pieces, then divide each of these into 3 different sized pieces; small, medium and large. Roll each of these pieces into finger-thick lengths and sit them in the moulds, joining the ends by squashing them together. When you have rolled all the pieces out and filled the moulds, you will have 6 moulds, each with 3 rings in increasing sizes.

3 Transfer the moulds to the heated oven and bake for 10 minutes, until golden. Leave to cool in the moulds until hardened, then remove from the moulds to a wire rack to cool completely.

4 To make the icing, whisk the egg whites in a large bowl until frothy. Add the icing sugar, a spoonful at a time, and fold in. Beat until very stiff and white, and it stands up in peaks. Spoon half of the icing into a separate bowl and colour with red colouring paste. Spoon this into a piping bag fitted with a small, plain writing nozzle. Spoon the white icing into a separate piping bag also fitted with a small, plain nozzle.

5 To assemble the kransekake, sort the cooked rings into decreasing sizes. Pipe a few dots of white icing onto the base of the largest ring and stick it on the centre of a large, round serving plate. Pipe the white and red icing in a zig-zag pattern around the ring and sprinkle with the edible glitter.

6 Place the next biggest ring on top of the iced ring (the piped icing will keep it in place) and pipe red and white icing in a zig-zag pattern as for the first ring, sprinkling with glitter. Repeat with the remaining rings, in decreasing size order, until you have a tower of 18 iced, glittery rings.

THE DAYS
IN BETWEEN

THE DAYS IN BETWEEN

The days in between 25th December and New Year's Eve are some of the loveliest as a quiet steals over the house and the preparations are over.

Boxing Day, the day after Christmas, was historically the day that service staff and tradesmen would receive their gifts or 'Christmas boxes' and have the day off – as they were required to work on Christmas Day itself. Today, this is when the leftover feasting begins in earnest and you can reap the benefits of having bought an extra-large turkey or ham.

Christmas wouldn't be complete without some classic leftover bakes such as a Turkey and Ham Pie (page 176), creamy pot pies and cobblers (pages 167 and 160) or a glorious Boxing Day Raised Pie (page 161). But you can be adventurous with all that remaining turkey too. Turkey Chilequiles (page 164) is a fantastic Mexican dish that will add spice and warmth to grey days. For those who love a baking challenge, the Turkey and Ham Chelsea Buns (page 171) are a fun twist on the usually sweet pastry.

For desserts at this stage of the festive season, try traditional classics like Sussex Pond Pudding (page 185) – so called because when you cut into it all the buttery, lemony juices come flooding out to form a pond around the pud – or an indulgent sticky toffee pudding. Or try something a little different like the Linzertorte (page 190), named after the city of Linz in Austria and often said to be the oldest cake in Europe, as it appears in a cookbook over 350 years old. With its sticky jam centre and light and crumbly nut based pastry, it is a perfect teatime accompaniment.

The joy of baking with leftovers is that you have all you need right there at your fingertips, so get experimenting and discover some delicious ideas for all that turkey, ham, stuffing and more.

CREAMY TURKEY AND TARRAGON COBBLER

A cobbler is a lovely alternative to a pie, with its light buttermilk scone topping. This is a fantastic leftover recipe, as you will have most of the ingredients already in your fridge from Christmas, so can pull it out of the hat in no time at all.

SERVES 4–6
YOU WILL NEED: A 2.5 LITRE OVENPROOF DISH

2 tablespoons olive oil

2 onions, finely chopped

4 garlic cloves, crushed

1 heaped tablespoon plain flour

200ml white wine

500ml chicken or turkey stock

175ml double cream

600g leftover turkey meat, shredded

2 tablespoons chopped fresh tarragon

2 tablespoons chopped fresh flat-leaf parsley

1 tablespoon Dijon mustard

300g frozen peas

a squeeze of lemon juice

salt and black pepper

For the cobbler

200g plain flour

1½ teaspoons baking powder

1 large egg, beaten

125ml buttermilk

1 Heat the oven to 200°C/400°F/gas 6. Heat the oil in a large pan over a medium heat. Add the onion and gently fry for 5 minutes, until soft. Add the garlic and cook for 1 further minute, then stir in the flour and cook for 30 seconds.

2 Stir in the wine and bubble for 1–2 minutes then add the stock and cream and bubble for 1 further minute. Add the turkey, herbs, mustard and frozen peas. Simmer for a couple of minutes then add the lemon juice, season to taste and set aside.

3 To make the cobbler, sift the flour and baking powder into a bowl and season. Add the beaten egg and buttermilk and mix together quickly to form a soft dough. Pour the creamy turkey into the ovenproof dish and dollop tablespoons of the cobbler mixture all over the top. Place in the heated oven and bake for 15–20 minutes, until the cobbler is risen and golden brown.

TIP

Try not to over-work the scone mixture for the cobbler or it will become heavy. Just bring the dough lightly together with your fingertips and it should stay light and airy.

PAUL'S HAND-RAISED BOXING DAY PIE

~~~~~~~~~~~~~~~~~~~~~~~~~~~~

SERVES 8–10
YOU WILL NEED: A 23CM ROUND SPRINGFORM CAKE TIN OR RAISED
PIE MOULD, LIBERALLY GREASED WITH MELTED LARD

For the pastry
450g plain flour, plus extra
   for dusting
100g strong white bread flour
1 teaspoon salt
75g chilled butter, cut into
   cubes

150g lard, cut into cubes
1 small egg, beaten, to glaze

For the filling
400g leftover stuffing (sage
   and onion, or your own
   preference)

500g cooked turkey, both
   white and brown meat,
   roughly chopped
200g fresh or frozen
   cranberries, defrosted
150g cranberry sauce
salt and black pepper

~~~~~~~~~~~~~~~~~~~~~~~~~~~~

1 Sift the flours and salt into a mixing bowl. Using your fingertips, rub the butter into the flour until the mixture resembles breadcrumbs. Make a well in the centre of the mixture.

2 Heat the lard and 200ml water in a small pan over a medium heat. When the mixture is simmering, pour it into the well in the flour and stir with a wooden spoon, gradually drawing the dry ingredients into the liquid, until the mixture comes together in a dough.

3 Knead the dough on a lightly floured surface until smooth and pliable. Roll out three-quarters of the dough and use to a line the prepared tin or mould. Press the pastry into the base and sides of the tin to prevent air bubbles from forming, leaving the excess hanging over the edge of the tin.

4 Spoon half of the stuffing into the pastry case and press down with the back of a spoon. Arrange half of the turkey over the stuffing, then season with salt and pepper. Mix the cranberries and cranberry sauce together and spoon half over

the turkey. Repeat the layers once more, pressing down as before.

5 Roll out the remaining pastry large enough to cover the pie. Brush the overhanging edges with water and place the lid on top, squeezing it together at the edges to seal. Trim off most of the excess pastry using scissors or a knife, and crimp using your fingers or the tines of a fork to create a decorative edge. Stamp out small stars from any leftover rolled out pastry, if you like, and use to decorate the top of the pie. Make a small hole in the centre of the lid and chill for 30 minutes. Heat the oven to 180°C/350°F/gas 4.

6 Place the pie in a roasting tin, transfer to the heated oven and cook for 45 minutes. Remove from the oven and brush with beaten egg to glaze. Return to the oven for 15 minutes.

7 Remove from the oven and leave to cool on a wire rack for 10 minutes. Cool for a further 30 minutes before removing the sides of the tin or mould.

Pictured overleaf

TURKEY CHILEQUILES

Add a bit of winter spice and sunshine to your leftovers with this Mexican dish. Usually made for breakfast or brunch to use up yesterday's tortilla, this more substantial version makes a great comfort-food supper.

~~~~~~~~~~~~~~~~~~~~~~~~~~~~~~~~

SERVES 4-6
YOU WILL NEED: A SHALLOW OVENPROOF DISH

1 onion, finely chopped

2 garlic cloves, sliced

2 green jalapeño chillies, finely sliced

1 x 400g tin of tomatillos (green tomatoes, see Tip)

a large handful of fresh coriander, chopped

50-100ml chicken stock

1 tablespoon vegetable oil

400g leftover turkey, shredded

250g tortilla chips

200ml soured cream

150g Lancashire cheese, grated

salt and black pepper

~~~~~~~~~~~~~~~~~~~~~~~~~~~~~~~~

1 Put the onion, garlic, chillies, tomatillos and coriander in a blender and whizz to a thick paste. Add enough of the stock to loosen the paste and whizz again. Season well.

2 Heat the oil in a pan and fry the paste for 5 minutes or until thickened slightly. Add the shredded turkey and toss well to combine.

3 Heat the oven to 180°C/350°F/gas 4. Layer up the tortilla chips with the turkey mixture in the ovenproof dish, adding dollops of soured cream and a scattering of grated cheese to each layer. Press down with your hands and finish with a scattering of cheese. Place in the heated oven and bake for 15-20 minutes until bubbling and the cheese is melted. Serve immediately.

TIP

Tomatillos are a type of green tomato found in Mexico. They have a unique flavour and are easy to buy online. If you can't find them, you could drain a can of cherry tomatoes of all its juice and mix them with the juice of a lime.

HAM AND STILTON POT PIES

This is a really flexible recipe – you could use turkey instead of ham, and different herbs, such as sage or thyme. Or swap the kale for spinach or even leftover sprouts. If you want to make one large pie, spoon all the filling into a 2 litre ovenproof dish and top with the pastry.

MAKES 6
YOU WILL NEED: 6 X 300ML RAMEKIN DISHES OR OVENPROOF POTS

200g kale or cavolo nero, shredded

25g unsalted butter

35g plain flour

225ml double cream

200ml ham or chicken stock

100g Stilton cheese, crumbled

2 teaspoons grainy mustard

a large handful of fresh flat-leaf parsley, finely chopped

600g leftover ham, shredded

1 small egg, mixed with 1 tablespoon milk

salt and black pepper

For the pastry

225g plain flour, plus extra for dusting

25g semolina

a good pinch of salt

125g chilled unsalted butter, cut into cubes

1 medium egg yolk

1–2 tablespoons cold water

1 To make the pastry, sift the flour, semolina and salt into a bowl, then rub in the butter with your fingertips (or use a food processor) until the mixture resembles breadcrumbs. Quickly mix in the egg yolk and just enough cold water to bring the dough together, then shape into a disc, wrap in clingfilm and chill.

2 Blanch the kale or cavolo nero in boiling water for 2–3 minutes, drain then refresh under cold water. Squeeze out as much excess water as you can and set aside.

3 Melt the butter in a pan, add the flour and cook, stirring, for 1–2 minutes. Mix the cream and stock together and gradually add, stirring constantly until you have a thick, smooth sauce. Increase the heat and bubble for a couple of minutes. Stir in the cheese and mustard. Check the seasoning and stir through the parsley, ham, and kale or cavolo nero. Divide between the ramekin dishes or ovenproof pots. Allow to cool. Heat the oven to 200°C/400°F/gas 6.

4 Roll out the pastry on a lightly floured surface to the thickness of a 50 pence coin and cut out 6 circles large enough to fit the top of your ramekins. Cut any trimmings into thin strips and stick these around the edge of each dish. Brush the trimmings with the beaten egg mixture and top with the discs of pastry, pressing well to seal. Make a small slit in the top of each pie. Brush again with the beaten egg mixture and place on a baking sheet. Transfer to the heated oven and bake for 25–30 minutes until golden brown.

HAM AND PARSLEY SAUCE PIE WITH BUBBLE AND SQUEAK MASH

Two classic dishes in one super-comfort dish. No sides are really needed here as it contains a bit of everything, but a winter leaf salad wouldn't go amiss.

~~~~~~~~~~

SERVES 6–8

YOU WILL NEED: A 2 LITRE OVENPROOF DISH

8 large floury potatoes (about 1kg), peeled and cut into chunks
75g full-fat cream cheese
25g Cheddar cheese, grated
100g unsalted butter
50g plain flour
300ml full-fat milk
50ml double cream

5–6 tablespoons very finely chopped fresh flat-leaf parsley
a good grating of fresh nutmeg
1 tablespoon olive oil
100g leftover cooked Brussels sprouts, sliced
4–5 spring onions, finely sliced
2 banana shallots, finely sliced

1 small leek, finely sliced
450g leftover cooked ham, torn into chunks
salt and black pepper

~~~~~~~~~~

1 Heat the oven to 200°C/400°F/gas 6. Place the potatoes in a pan of cold, salted water and bring to the boil. Simmer gently for 12–15 minutes until tender, then drain well. Return to the pan over a low heat and mash well with 25g of the cream cheese, the Cheddar and 25g of the butter. Remove from the heat and set aside.

2 Meanwhile, melt 50g of the butter in a pan and add the flour. Cook for a couple of minutes then gradually add the milk, stirring, until you have a smooth sauce. Season and bubble away for 1–2 minutes then add the cream, remaining cream cheese, the parsley and nutmeg, and remove from the heat.

3 Heat the oil in a pan over a medium heat and fry the sliced sprouts and spring onions for 1 minute, then add to the mash and mix well. Season and set aside.

4 Heat the remaining 25g butter and gently fry the shallot and leek for 5 minutes until tender. Toss the ham through and mix all of this with the sauce. Tip into an ovenproof dish and top with the mash. Place in the heated oven and bake for 25–30 minutes until the mash is golden brown and the pie bubbling.

PAUL'S TURKEY, STUFFING AND CRANBERRY CHELSEA BUNS

SERVES 10–12
YOU WILL NEED: A LARGE, DEEP-SIDED BAKING TRAY OR ROASTING TIN, BUTTERED

For the dough
500g strong white bread flour, plus extra for dusting
50g caster sugar
40g unsalted butter, plus extra for greasing
2 medium eggs
2 x 7g sachets fast-action dried yeast

10g salt
150ml warm milk

1 x 270g jar of cranberry sauce
300g leftover roast turkey, shredded
200g leftover sage and onion stuffing

1 Place all the dough ingredients in a large bowl with 140ml water. Stir with your hands until a dough is formed, then slowly add 50ml more water and massage the dough in the bowl for 4 minutes.

2 Tip the dough onto a lightly floured surface and knead well for 10 minutes, until smooth and elastic. Place back in the bowl and leave to rise for 1 hour, covered with a damp tea towel.

3 Tip the risen dough out onto a very lightly floured surface and roll out to a rectangle about 50 x 25cm and 5mm thick. Spread the cranberry sauce onto the surface of the dough, using a palette knife, then sprinkle the turkey and stuffing on top.

4 Roll up the dough quite tightly towards you, starting with the long side furthest from you. Use a sharp knife to cut the rolled dough into 5cm thick rounds. Place cut side up in the buttered baking tray or roasting tin, spacing them 1cm apart (you want them to be touching once cooked), cover with a tea towel and leave to rise in a warm place for 1 hour. Heat the oven to 200°C/400°F/gas 6.

5 Place the risen buns in the heated oven and bake for 15–20 minutes, until golden brown. Leave to cool in the tin for a few minutes, then transfer to a wire rack.

HAM AND CHESTNUT PASTA BAKE

Use any shaped pasta you have in your cupboard for this simple dish, and experiment with the flavours, using wine instead of cider, cream instead of crème fraîche and turkey or chicken instead of ham, or a mixture of the two to use up more leftovers.

SERVES 6
YOU WILL NEED: A 2 LITRE OVENPROOF DISH

1 tablespoon olive oil

a knob of unsalted butter

1 onion, finely chopped

2 garlic cloves, finely chopped

a few sprigs of fresh thyme, leaves stripped

1 teaspoon fennel seeds

2 tablespoons plain flour

250ml cider

150ml hot chicken stock

300ml crème fraîche

500g leftover ham, shredded or roughly chopped

200g cooked peeled chestnuts, roughly chopped

a small handful of fresh flat-leaf parsley, leaves chopped

400g penne dried pasta

5 tablespoons fresh breadcrumbs

60g Parmesan cheese, grated

salt and black pepper

1 Heat the oil and butter in a large saucepan and gently fry the onion over a low heat for 10 minutes until softened. Add the garlic, thyme and fennel seeds and cook for 1 further minute, then stir in the flour and cook for 30 seconds.

2 Add the cider and bubble away until reduced by half, then stir in the hot stock and crème fraîche. Season well and add the ham, chestnuts and parsley. Simmer for 1–2 minutes then set aside.

3 Heat the oven to 200°C/400°F/gas 6. Cook the pasta in a large pan of boiling, slightly salted water for 10 minutes, until just cooked, then drain well.

4 Mix the drained pasta into the sauce and tip into an ovenproof dish. Mix the breadcrumbs with the Parmesan and scatter all over the top of the dish, then place in the heated oven and bake for 15 minutes until golden and bubbling. Leave to stand for 10 minutes before serving with garlic bread and a bitter leaf salad.

TURKEY AND HAM PIE

There is nothing more warming than a turkey and ham pie and this one comes with a topping of golden flaky mashed potato pastry. The addition of mash transforms everyday shortcrust into something altogether more indulgent.

SERVES 4–6
YOU WILL NEED: A 1.5 LITRE PIE DISH; A PIE FUNNEL

3 tablespoons olive oil
15g butter
1 large onion, finely chopped
2 garlic cloves, crushed
1 teaspoon caraway seeds
1 tablespoon plain flour
400g leftover turkey, shredded
200g leftover ham, cut into small pieces
125ml medium-dry sherry

250ml turkey or chicken stock, or leftover turkey gravy mixed with water or stock
75ml crème fraîche
2 tablespoons finely chopped fresh tarragon
3 tablespoons finely chopped fresh flat-leaf parsley
1 small egg, beaten with 1 tablespoon milk
salt and black pepper

For the pastry
1 large baking potato (about 200g) OR 100g leftover mashed potato
200g plain flour, plus extra for dusting
a good pinch of salt
100g cold unsalted butter, cubed
25g cold lard
1 medium egg yolk

1 To make the pastry, heat the oven to 200°C/400°F/gas 6, if using a baking potato, and bake the potato for 1 hour until tender. Halve, scoop out the flesh and mash with a fork, then cool. Sift the flour and salt into a bowl. Quickly rub the butter and lard into the flour with your fingertips until it resembles breadcrumbs (you can do this in a food processor if you prefer).

2 Mix in the cooled or leftover mashed potato. Quickly mix in the egg yolk until the mixture just starts to come together, then knead briefly on a lightly floured work surface. Shape into a disc, wrap in clingfilm and chill for 20–30 minutes.

3 Heat the oil and butter in a large frying pan and gently fry the onion for 10 minutes until softened. Add the garlic and caraway seeds and cook for 1 minute, then stir in the flour for 30 seconds. Add the meat, then the sherry, chicken stock and crème fraîche. Season well and bring to

a simmer. Stir in the herbs, then leave to cool. Spoon the cooled mixture into the pie dish and nestle a pie funnel into the centre. Heat the oven to 200°C/400°F/gas 6 if it isn't hot from baking the potato.

4 Roll out the pastry on a lightly floured surface until it is a little larger than the dish and about 3mm thick. Brush the rim of the pie dish with a little of the beaten egg mixture, then cover the dish with the pastry, cutting a small slit to allow the pie funnel to poke through. If you don't have a pie funnel, cut 2 or 3 small slits in the pastry to allow steam to escape. Roughly trim and crimp the edges, either with your fingers or a fork.

5 Brush the pastry all over with the beaten egg mixture, then re-roll the trimmings and cut out decorations for the top. Brush with more egg, then place in the heated oven and bake for 25–30 minutes until golden brown.

SMOKED SALMON, FENNEL AND HORSERADISH TART WITH CARAWAY PASTRY

If you are not overly keen on caraway, and some people aren't, you can leave it out of the pastry; you will still get a lovely aniseedy flavour from the fennel, but in a much more subtle way.

SERVES 8
YOU WILL NEED: A 23CM FLUTED, 2.5CM DEEP TART TIN

2 tablespoons olive oil
25g unsalted butter
1 onion, finely sliced
1 large fennel bulb, very finely sliced
1 tablespoon freshly grated horseradish
1 large egg and 2 large yolks

200ml crème fraîche
50ml double cream
juice of ½ lemon
2 tablespoons finely chopped fresh flat-leaf parsley
200g sustainable smoked salmon, sliced
salt and black pepper

For the pastry
120g unsalted butter, diced
200g plain flour, plus extra for dusting
1 teaspoon caraway seeds
a good pinch of salt
2 tablespoons ice-cold water

1 To make the pastry, rub the butter into the flour in a bowl, using your fingertips, until the mixture resembles breadcrumbs. Add the caraway seeds and salt, then add the water a little at a time, mixing with a flat-bladed knife, until the pastry just starts to come together. Bring it together with your hands and knead briefly on a lightly floured surface until smooth. Shape into a disc, wrap in clingfilm and chill for 20 minutes. Meanwhile, heat the oven to 200°C/400°F/gas 6.

2 Roll out the pastry on a lightly floured surface and use to line the tart tin. Line the pastry with baking paper and fill with ceramic baking beans or rice, then place in the heated oven and blind bake for 12 minutes. Remove the baking paper and beans and return the tart case to the oven for a further 5 minutes, until lightly golden. Reduce the oven temperature to 180°C/350°F/gas 4.

3 Meanwhile, heat the oil and butter in a pan and gently fry the onion and fennel over a low heat for 20 minutes, until lovely and soft. Add the horseradish and cook for a further 5 minutes. Season well and set aside to cool.

4 In a jug, mix the whole egg, egg yolks, crème fraîche, cream and lemon juice. Add the parsley and season well. Mix the cooled onion and fennel mixture with the smoked salmon and spread evenly into the pastry case. Pour over the egg and cream mixture, transfer to the heated oven and bake for 20–25 minutes until set. Allow to cool in the tin for 10 minutes before removing and serving.

TIP

If you can't get fresh horseradish, use 2 tablespoons creamed hot horseradish instead.

APPLE AND SAGE STUFFING SAUSAGE ROLLS WITH CRACKLING PASTRY

Here is about as fine a sausage roll as you could wish for, with the addition of crackling on the crust giving it an extra twist. If you have any leftover raw sausagemeat stuffing from your turkey, you can keep it to make this filling. For nibble-sized rolls, just cut them into smaller pieces before baking.

MAKES 6 LARGE SAUSAGE ROLLS

450g sausagemeat
50g fresh breadcrumbs
50ml cider
1 tablespoon finely chopped
    fresh sage
a small handful of fresh
    flat-leaf parsley, finely
    chopped

1 small eating apple, cored
    and grated
2 teaspoons Dijon mustard
500g block of all-butter puff
    pastry, thawed if frozen
plain flour, for dusting
1 medium egg, lightly beaten
30g pork scratchings, crushed
salt and black pepper

1 Mix together the sausagemeat, breadcrumbs, cider, herbs, apple and mustard in a big bowl. Season well.

2 Cut the pastry in half and roll out each half on a lightly floured surface to a 36 x 18cm rectangle. Divide the sausagemeat mixture in half, roll each portion into a 40cm-long sausage shape and place one along the middle of each pastry strip. Brush the edges of the pastry with a little beaten egg, then fold over to enclose the filling, and seal well. Trim off any excess pastry at the join and

chill for 10 minutes. Heat the oven to 220°C/425°F/gas 7.

3 Brush the pastry all over with more egg and press the pork scratchings all over the top. With a sharp knife, cut each into 3 individual sausage rolls and place on a baking sheet.

4 Put in the heated oven and bake for 20–25 minutes until golden and puffed, and the filling is cooked. Cool on a wire rack for 10 minutes before serving warm.

BLUE CHEESE, PEAR AND WALNUT TART WITH WATERCRESS PESTO

Pears are delicious as part of this savoury dish, as their natural sweetness goes so well with rich blue cheese and spicy watercress. Any leftover pesto can be mixed with a good dollop of cream or cream cheese and stirred through just-cooked pasta.

SERVES 6–8

a knob of unsalted butter

2 tablespoons white balsamic vinegar

2 firm, ripe pears, cut into wedges

75g watercress, plus a handful of extra leaves to garnish

a small handful of fresh flat-leaf parsley

1 garlic clove, crushed

25g pine nuts

25g grated Parmesan cheese

50ml olive oil (use half extra virgin if you like)

375g sheet of ready-rolled all-butter puff pastry, thawed if frozen

125g blue cheese, such as Stilton, crumbled

a handful of walnuts, roughly chopped

salt and black pepper

1 Heat the oven to 200°C/400°F/gas 6. Melt the butter in a pan with the vinegar, add the pears and cook for 2 minutes on each side until caramelised, then remove from the heat and lightly season.

2 To make the pesto, whizz the watercress, parsley, garlic and pine nuts in a food processor. Add the grated Parmesan then, with the motor running, gradually pour in the oil until you have a thick, glossy pesto. If it is a little too thick, you can add a little water to loosen it.

3 Unroll the pastry sheet and score a border 2cm in from the edge. Place on a baking sheet and arrange the pears over the pastry within the border. Scatter over the crumbled cheese and walnuts.

4 Put in the heated oven and bake for 15 minutes until the pastry is puffed and golden and the cheese is melted and bubbling. Slip onto a serving plate or board, drizzle with the pesto, scatter with extra watercress leaves and serve.

HOLLY'S HAM AND CHUTNEY LEFTOVER TURNOVERS

I love leftovers at Christmas time, but sometimes they need a little helping hand to present them to guests. These are easy to make, get gobbled up in minutes and taste great hot or cold. I'd consider adding a little crumbled cheese to the pastry too if you have any lingering in the fridge. Be careful if eating them hot as the sugar in the chutney is very hot.

MAKES ABOUT 12
YOU WILL NEED: AN 11CM ROUND PLAIN CUTTER (OR A LARGE GLASS)

100g tomato chutney, or any chutney of your choice

320g leftover ham, cut into 1cm chunks

1 egg, beaten with a pinch of salt

For the pastry
280g plain flour, plus extra for dusting

1 teaspoon freshly ground black pepper

140g cold, unsalted butter, cut into cubes

about 4 tablespoons iced water

1 To make the pastry, sift the flour into a bowl, add the black pepper and stir well. Rub the butter into the flour with your fingertips until the mixture resembles breadcrumbs. Using a blunt knife, stir in enough iced water for the pastry to just come together (you may not need all of it, depending on the flour you use and the humidity in the kitchen). Gather the pastry with your hands, shape into a disc, wrap in clingfilm and chill for 1 hour. Meanwhile, heat the oven to 200°C/400°F/gas 6 and line a baking sheet with baking paper.

2 Roll out the chilled pastry on a lightly floured surface to a 2–3mm thickness. Use an 11cm round cutter, or a large glass if you don't have one, to cut out as many circles as you can. Re-roll the trimmings to make more circles.

3 Holding a pastry circle in your hand, spread 1 teaspoon chutney on one side, then add some ham. Use a pastry brush or your finger to dampen the edge of the pastry with the beaten egg. Fold in half and pinch the edges together to seal. Place on the lined baking sheet and brush the top with egg wash.

4 Repeat until all the pastry circles and filling are used up, then put in the heated oven and bake for 15–20 minutes until golden brown. Some of the filling may escape, but they will still taste great!

ST. STEPHEN'S DAY MUFFINS

St. Stephen's Day is the Irish holiday that we more typically call Boxing Day.
As to be expected, 26th December marks the start of enjoying all the leftovers
from the previous two days, and these boozy muffins are no exception.

MAKES 8
YOU WILL NEED: A 12-HOLE MUFFIN TIN, LINED WITH 8 MUFFIN CASES

190g plain flour
2 teaspoons baking powder
1–2 teaspoons ground mixed
 spice
115g light muscovado sugar
2 medium eggs

115ml milk
45g unsalted butter, melted
3 tablespoons sweet sherry
200g leftover Christmas
 pudding, crumbled
icing sugar, for dusting

1 Heat the oven to 180°C/350°F/gas 4.

2 Mix together the flour, baking powder, mixed spice and sugar in a bowl. Whisk together the eggs, milk, melted butter and sherry in a jug or bowl, then pour into the dry ingredients with the crumbled Christmas pudding and stir briefly to form a slightly lumpy batter.

3 Divide the batter between the muffin cases, place in the heated oven and bake for 20–25 minutes until risen and golden, and a skewer inserted into the centre of one comes out clean.

4 Remove to a wire rack to cool and dust with icing sugar before serving.

SUSSEX POND PUDDING

Sharp and tangy lemon encased in a rich suet crust, Sussex pond is a truly classic British pud, so-called because when you cut into it all the buttery lemon juices fill the plate like a pond. Make sure you have a plate with a good lip to catch all the sauce as it pours forth.

SERVES 6

YOU WILL NEED: A 1.2 LITRE PUDDING BASIN, BUTTERED

2 large unwaxed lemons
250g self-raising flour, plus
  extra for dusting
115g suet
100ml full-fat milk

100g cold butter, cut into
  cubes, plus extra for
  greasing
100g caster sugar

1 Prick the lemons all over with a skewer. Mix the flour and suet in a bowl. Add the milk and 50ml water and bring it together into a dough. Cut off one-third of the dough and set aside.

2 Roll out the larger piece of dough on a lightly floured surface and use it to line the buttered pudding basin.

3 Add half the cold butter cubes and half the sugar to the dough-lined bowl. Pop the whole lemons on top, then top with the rest of the butter and sugar. Roll out the smaller piece of dough to make a lid that fits the top of the pudding basin (this will become the base, so make it nice and thick). Brush the edges of the pastry lid with water, put on top of the pudding and press all around the edges to seal together.

4 Cover the basin with a piece of baking paper, pleated across the centre, and tie it securely under the rim of the basin with string. Before cutting the string, take it up over the top to create a loose handle, then tie securely. Trim off any excess baking paper so it doesn't trail in the water and let moisture in.

5 Place the basin in a large pan and pour in boiling water to reach two-thirds of the way up the sides of the pudding basin. Cover with a lid and simmer very gently, topping up the water every so often, for 3½ hours.

6 Remove from the heat and allow the pudding to rest for 10 minutes before removing the string and baking paper and carefully turning the pudding out onto a lipped serving plate or dish. When serving, ensure everyone gets a little of the lemon.

TIP

Try to look for lemons with thin skins rather than thick, knobbly ones, as these will cook down more for a more tender result.

STICKY TOFFEE PUDDING

A childhood classic that is still going strong, sticky toffee is a real man's pudding – dense, fudgy and sweet. It is, without doubt, a king of puddings.

SERVES 6
YOU WILL NEED: A 2.5 LITRE OVENPROOF DISH, BUTTERED

185g medjool dates, stones removed, finely chopped
300ml boiling water
1 teaspoon bicarbonate of soda
80g butter, softened, plus extra for greasing
70g caster sugar
80g dark muscovado sugar
2 medium eggs, lightly beaten

185g self-raising flour
1 teaspoon baking powder
½ teaspoon ground allspice
50g pecans, roughly chopped

For the toffee sauce
125g unsalted butter
75g dark muscovado sugar
45g caster sugar
1 teaspoon vanilla extract
200ml double cream

1 Heat the oven to 180°C/350°F/gas 4. Put the dates in a bowl and cover with the boiling water. Sprinkle in the bicarbonate of soda and set aside for 10 minutes.

2 Beat the butter and sugars together with an electric mixer until light and fluffy. Gradually whisk in the eggs, beating well between each addition. Sift over the flour, baking powder and allspice and fold in with the pecans. Stir the dates in their bowl, add with their soaking liquid to the cake mixture, and mix together well. The mixture will be very wet but don't worry.

3 Pour into the prepared dish, place in the heated oven and bake for 30–35 minutes until the sponge is just coming away from the sides of the dish.

4 Meanwhile, to make the sauce, melt the butter in a heavy-based pan. Add the sugars and vanilla, then stir well until the sugar has dissolved. Add the cream and bring up to a vigorous simmer, then bubble for 5 minutes.

5 Once the sponge is cooked, remove from the oven and heat the grill to medium. Make little holes all over the sponge with a skewer, then pour over the hot toffee sauce. Pop under the grill for 30 seconds, watching it like a hawk to make sure it doesn't catch and burn, then cool for 5 minutes before serving with cream or vanilla ice cream.

PANETTONE BREAD AND BUTTER PUDDING

Panettone is a wonderfully fragranced bread, delicious for breakfast, but it goes
stale very quickly, so this is a fantastic way of using up any that is past its best.
If you don't have a panettone to hand, you could use bread, croissants or brioche,
adding a good handful of raisins, sultanas and mixed peel.

~~~~~~

SERVES 6-8
YOU WILL NEED: A 2 LITRE OVENPROOF DISH, BUTTERED; A ROASTING TIN

750g stale panettone
75g unsalted butter, softened,
   plus extra for greasing
4-5 tablespoons brandy or
   dark rum

4 large eggs
25g caster sugar
450ml full-fat milk
300ml double cream
1 teaspoon vanilla extract

~~~~~~

1 Slice the panettone into thin wedges and lightly butter one side of each. Arrange in the buttered ovenproof dish, buttered side up, in a single, overlapping layer. Drizzle with the brandy or rum.

2 Mix together the eggs and sugar in a large bowl, then whisk in the milk, cream and vanilla. Pour evenly over the top of the panettone slices and leave to stand for at least 30 minutes. Meanwhile, heat the oven to 170°C/325°F/gas 3.

3 Place the baking dish in a roasting tin and pour enough just-boiled water into the tin to come halfway up the sides of the baking dish. Transfer to the heated oven and bake for 35-40 minutes until the custard is just set and the pudding puffed up and golden. Remove from the oven and allow to rest for 10 minutes before serving with double cream.

LINZERTORTE

An Austrian recipe dating back hundreds of years, this latticed bake – a little like a spiced jam tart – has many versions, but all have a nutty, very crumbly base of hazelnuts or almonds with a rich, jammy filling. Redcurrant jam is traditionally used, but as it is hard to find outside Austria, this recipe uses a mixture of redcurrant jelly and raspberry jam.

SERVES 10–12
YOU WILL NEED: A 30 X 20CM FLUTED, RECTANGULAR,
LOOSE-BOTTOMED TART TIN, GREASED

3 tablespoons dry, fine breadcrumbs

8 tablespoons each of redcurrant jelly and raspberry jam

1 medium egg yolk, beaten with 1 teaspoon water, for glazing

For the crust

150g finely ground hazelnuts (see Tip)

275g plain flour, plus extra for dusting

1 teaspoon ground cinnamon

a pinch of ground cloves

½ teaspoon salt

225g cold unsalted butter, cut into cubes

85g icing sugar

2 medium egg yolks

finely grated zest of 1 lemon and a squeeze of juice

1 To make the crust, mix the ground hazelnuts, flour, ground spices and salt in a bowl. Add the butter and, with your fingertips, rub into the flour mixture until it resembles breadcrumbs. Add the icing sugar, stir well, then quickly mix in the egg yolks, lemon zest and a squeeze of juice so it starts to come together.

2 Turn out onto a lightly floured surface and knead briefly until smooth. Remove one-third of the dough. Shape the smaller piece into a disc, wrap in clingfilm and chill in the fridge for 10 minutes. Meanwhile, heat the oven to 180°C/350°F/gas 4.

3 Roll out the remaining dough on a lightly floured surface into a rectangle large enough to line the tart tin. Lift into the tin and press into an even layer over the base and sides, patching any gaps, as the dough is very crumbly. Add any trimmings to the pastry disc in the fridge. Chill the base for 10 minutes.

4 Place the base in the heated oven and bake for 10–15 minutes until it has barely begun to colour, then set aside to cool. While the base is baking, roll out the remaining dough between 2 sheets of non-stick baking paper into a rectangle about 32 x 22cm, then return to the fridge and chill for 20 minutes.

5 Sprinkle the cooked base of the torte with the breadcrumbs, then spoon the redcurrant jelly and raspberry jam evenly over the top (spoon on in blobs, and then use a palette knife to spread them out).

6 Remove the chilled pastry from the fridge and take off the sheets of baking paper. Cut the pastry into strips, about 1.5 cm wide, across the diagonal (if you have a fluted pastry wheel you can create a lovely crimped edge to your strips). Lay these one at a time over the jam, using a long spatula as the pastry is crumbly,

CONTINUED

to make a criss-cross lattice pattern. Neaten any excess pastry at the edges by pressing it against the side of the tin.

7 Brush the pastry with the egg glaze, put in the heated oven and bake for 45–50 minutes until golden all over. Allow to cool for 10 minutes before removing from the tin. Cut into portions and serve.

TIP

To grind hazelnuts without them turning oily, place them in a food processor with half of the flour and pulse together until the hazelnuts are finely ground into the flour. If you want you can continue to make the pastry in the food processor.

MARY'S GALETTE

~~~~~~

MAKES 1 LARGE TART

750g block of all-butter puff
  pastry, chilled
plain flour, for dusting
1 small egg, beaten

For the filling
100g unsalted butter, softened
100g caster sugar
1 large egg and 1 large yolk,
  at room temperature

100g ground almonds
50g flaked almonds
1 teaspoon almond extract

~~~~~~

1 Line a baking sheet with non-stick baking paper. Roll out half the pastry on a lightly floured surface until slightly thinner than a £1 coin. Cut out a round about 23cm in diameter, place on the lined baking sheet and cover with clingfilm. Roll out the remaining pastry in the same way and cut out a second round the same size. Set this on top of the clingfilm, then cover the whole lot with clingfilm. Chill while you make the filling.

2 Beat the butter until creamy, using a wooden spoon or hand-held electric mixer. Beat in the sugar, then beat thoroughly until pale and fluffy. Beat the egg with the yolk until just combined, then gradually add to the butter mixture a tablespoonful at a time, beating well after each addition. When the mixture is very light in colour and texture, gently stir in the ground almonds, flaked almonds and almond extract. Cover the bowl and chill for 15–20 minutes.

3 Uncover the pastry, remove the top pastry round and the clingfilm. Spoon the filling onto the pastry round on the baking sheet, mounding it slightly in the middle and leaving a clear 2cm border all around the edge.

4 Brush the pastry border with beaten egg, then gently lay the second pastry round over the filling. Press the edges firmly together to seal. Holding a small knife blade at right angles to the side of the pastry, 'knock up' the edge all around by making small indentations in the pastry. Then scallop the edge by pulling the indentations in at 2cm intervals with the back of the knife. Brush the top of the pastry very lightly with beaten egg and chill for 20 minutes. Meanwhile, heat the oven to 220°C/425°F/gas 7.

5 Brush the top a second time with the egg glaze, then score a pattern on top, using the tip of a sharp knife. Make a couple of small steam holes in the centre, place in the heated oven and bake for 25–30 minutes or until the pastry is golden brown and crisp. Leave to cool slightly before serving.

STICKY CLEMENTINE AND STAR ANISE DRIZZLE LOAF

Leftover clementines languishing in a bowl are transformed into a fabulously moist and fragranced syrup cake. It would make a fantastic pudding as well as being perfect with a cup of tea.

MAKES 12 SLICES
YOU WILL NEED: A 450G LOAF TIN, GREASED AND LINED

175g unsalted butter,
    softened, plus extra for
    greasing
175g caster sugar
finely grated zest of 1 lemon
    and 4 clementines
3 medium eggs
125g self-raising flour

50g ground almonds
a splash of milk

For the syrup
100g caster sugar
juice of 1 lemon and 4
    clementines (see above)
2 star anise

1 Heat the oven to 180°C/350°F/gas 4. Beat together the butter, sugar and citrus zests using a hand-held electric whisk until really light and fluffy. Add the eggs, one at a time, beating until well combined before adding the next.

2 Fold in the flour and ground almonds until you have a smooth mixture, adding just enough milk to make it a dropping consistency (so that it falls off the spoon), then dollop into the prepared tin and level the top. Place in the heated oven and bake for about 50–55 minutes, until a skewer comes out just dry.

3 Meanwhile, to make the syrup, put the sugar, citrus juices and star anise in a pan and place over a low heat. Once the sugar has melted, bubble for a couple of minutes to a thin syrup

– the mixture should feel a little greasy when you rub it between your fingertips. Set aside off the heat to infuse while the cake is cooking, then strain into a jug.

4 Pierce the cake all over with a skewer when it comes out of the oven and pour over the syrup. Allow to stand in the tin until all of the syrup has been absorbed into the sponge and the cake is cool. Remove from the tin and serve.

TIP

There might seem like a lot of syrup for a small cake, but be patient and pour it slowly, and it will all soak in to make a gorgeously sticky treat.

RUTH'S CHRISTMAS BAKEWELL TART

This is a twist on the classic mince pie and is guaranteed to go down a treat with friends and family. Perfect served cold or slightly warmed with a good dollop of brandy cream.

SERVES 10
YOU WILL NEED: A 20CM FLUTED, DEEP-SIDED TIN, BUTTERED

1 x 400g jar of mincemeat
200g ground almonds
100g semolina
150g caster sugar
150g butter, melted and
  slightly cooled, plus extra
  for greasing
3 large eggs

a few drops of almond extract
75g icing sugar

For the pastry
225g plain flour, plus extra
  for dusting
125g cold butter, diced
50g caster sugar
1–3 tablespoons chilled water

1 To make the pastry, put the flour in a large bowl. Add the diced butter and rub into the flour with your fingertips until the mixture resembles fine breadcrumbs. Stir through the sugar and add the chilled water 1 tablespoon at a time, mixing gently until the pastry comes together. Knead lightly until even, wrap in clingfilm and chill in the fridge for 30 minutes. Meanwhile, heat the oven to 180°C/350°C/gas 4.

2 Roll out the chilled pastry on a lightly floured surface to a 3mm thickness and use to line the prepared tin, neatly trimming any excess from the edges.

3 Spoon the mincemeat onto the pastry base and roughly level it out. Combine the ground almonds, semolina and caster sugar in a bowl.

Add the melted butter, eggs and almond extract, then stir well until the mixture is evenly combined.

4 Pour over the top of the mincemeat, place in the heated oven and bake for 1 hour, or until golden and springy to the touch. Remove from the oven and allow to cool before removing the tart from the tin.

5 Make a thick icing by adding 2–3 teaspoons water to the icing sugar, beating well. Drizzle this in a decorative criss-cross pattern over the top of the tart, and serve.

THINKING AHEAD

The bakewell tart can be frozen before the icing is added. Defrost at room temperature and ice when ready.

NEW YEAR'S EVE

NEW YEAR'S EVE

New Year's Eve brings with it lots of culinary traditions for fortune and prosperity for the coming year.

In Spain, it is the custom to eat twelve grapes, one on each stroke of midnight, to bring luck for the coming twelve months. Lentils and pulses are thought to resemble coins and are eaten for wealth and prosperity in many different countries, and in the Netherlands, ring-shaped foods are eaten as a symbol that the year has come full circle.

In Scotland, New Year's Eve, or Hogmanay as it is known, is celebrated with the tradition of first footing. After the clock strikes twelve, to ensure food, warmth and wealth for the coming year, the first foot over the threshold should belong to a dark-haired man bearing gifts of a piece of coal, shortbread, whisky and in more recent years, a freshly baked Black Bun (page 223). The Haggis Scotch Eggs on page 210 are a nod to the traditional Hogmanay dinner, but also make a wonderful party nibble.

New Year's Eve is undoubtedly the biggest party night of the year. Baking is key to a good feast, as so much can be done well in advance to leave you free to enjoy your own party. Canapés and small bites are ideal, especially if you have a lot of guests, as you can have them ready on trays to cook through the evening. This chapter includes crisp Mushroom, Spinach and Feta Parcels (page 204), Parma Ham and Gruyère Palmiers (page 208) or light Cheesy Gougères (page 209) which all go down well with a glass of New Year's fizz. And of course, a dessert, such as the Passion Fruit and Pomegranate Pavlova Layer Cake (page 225) makes a showstopping centrepiece, and is a spectacular way to see in the New Year.

MUSHROOM, SPINACH AND FETA PARCELS

Warm, crisp and golden parcels filled with cheese and spinach will be gobbled up by hungry hordes in moments. Try different fillings, using goats' cheese instead of feta, or mix the mushrooms with cream cheese and lots of parsley.

MAKES 20

300g baby spinach
2 tablespoons olive oil
25g butter, plus 75g, melted
150g white mushrooms, finely chopped
150g feta cheese, crumbled

a small bunch of fresh dill, finely chopped
a good grating of nutmeg
5 sheets of filo pastry (40 x 30cm)
salt and black pepper

1 Wilt the spinach by pouring over a kettle of boiling water, then drain and refresh under cold running water. Squeeze out as much water as possible, then roughly chop and tip into a bowl.

2 Heat the oil in a pan with the 25g butter and fry the mushrooms over a high heat until golden all over. Add to the spinach in the bowl and allow to cool, then add the feta, dill and nutmeg. Season well and set aside. Meanwhile, heat the oven to 200°C/400°F/gas 6.

3 Cut 1 sheet of filo lengthways into 7.5cm wide strips and brush all over with melted butter, keeping the rest of the filo sheets under a slightly damp tea towel until you need them.

4 Put 1 tablespoonful of the filling mixture at one end of a strip of pastry in the middle and fold one of the top corners over the filling, enclosing it in a triangle shape. Fold the triangle up along the strip to seal the filling, then keep folding until you reach the end and have a neat triangle parcel. Brush all over with melted butter and transfer to a baking sheet. Repeat with the remaining filo strips, sheets and filling; you will only need half the last sheet of filo.

5 Brush the triangle parcels all over with more butter, place in the heated oven and bake for 15–20 minutes until golden brown.

STILTON AND BACON MUFFINS

These flavoursome savoury muffins are quick and easy to make
but delicious and moreish – perfect for serving at a party.

MAKES 12

YOU WILL NEED: A 12-HOLE MUFFIN TIN, LINED WITH MUFFIN CASES

1 tablespoon vegetable oil
240g smoked bacon, chopped
250g plain flour
½ teaspoon coarse sea salt
2 teaspoons baking powder
½ teaspoon bicarbonate
   of soda
90g Stilton cheese, crumbled

2 medium eggs
75g unsalted butter, melted
   and cooled
250ml buttermilk
a bunch of fresh chives,
   snipped
black pepper

1 Heat the oven to 200°C/400°F/gas 6. Heat the oil in a frying pan and fry the bacon for 3–4 minutes until crispy. Remove with a slotted spoon and set aside on kitchen paper.

2 Mix the flour, salt, baking powder, bicarbonate of soda and crumbled Stilton in a large bowl. Beat the eggs, butter, buttermilk and chives together in a jug, and season with lots of pepper.

3 Pour the egg mixture over the dry ingredients and stir until just combined. Fold in the cooled bacon until everything is evenly distributed but the batter is still lumpy. It is important not to over-mix.

4 Spoon the batter equally between the muffin cases, place the tin in the heated oven and bake for 18–20 minutes until golden and risen, or until a skewer inserted into the centre of one muffin comes out clean. Remove the muffins from the tin and place on a cooling rack until ready to serve.

PARMA HAM AND GRUYÈRE PALMIERS

So simple to make, these addictive little moustache-shaped bites are the ultimate nibble for New Year's Eve. Make lots, as they will disappear in a flash.

MAKES ABOUT 45

375g sheet of ready-rolled all-butter puff pastry, thawed if frozen
1 tablespoon Dijon or English mustard

25g Gruyère cheese, grated
25g Parmesan cheese, grated
3–4 slices Parma ham
1 small egg, lightly beaten
oil, for greasing

1 Unroll the pastry sheet and cut in half lengthways. Spread both halves evenly with mustard, leaving a 1cm border around each edge. Sprinkle with the cheeses then top with the slices of Parma ham.

2 Roll up each long side of one sheet to halfway so they meet in the middle. Do the same for the other, then brush both all over with the beaten egg and chill in the fridge for at least 1 hour.

3 Heat the oven to 200°C/400°F/gas 6. Cut the chilled rolls into slices about 7mm thick, then arrange on 2 large baking sheets, greased, leaving a small gap between each, as they will spread a little as they cook. Transfer to the heated oven and bake for 8–10 minutes until golden and puffed. Serve warm.

TIP

These will keep in an airtight tin for a day or two – just warm through in a medium oven to crisp them up again.

THINKING AHEAD

To make the palmiers ahead of time, freeze the rolled-up whole (see step 2) then cut off as much as you want. Brush with beaten egg, slice into rounds and cook from frozen in a hot oven (see step 3).

REALLY CHEESY GOUGÈRES

No one can resist these little bites of warm, cheesy choux pastry.
The triple cheese makes them extra moreish, so be sure to make plenty of them.

MAKES 30–35
YOU WILL NEED: A PIPING BAG FITTED WITH A LARGE, PLAIN NOZZLE

150ml full-fat milk
50g unsalted butter
¼ teaspoon cayenne pepper
75g plain flour
2 large eggs

30g Stilton cheese, crumbled
30g Parmesan cheese, grated,
    plus extra to sprinkle
45g Cheddar cheese, grated
salt and black pepper

1 Heat the oven to 220°C/425°F/gas 7 and line 2 baking sheets with non-stick baking paper.

2 Put the milk and butter in a saucepan with plenty of salt and pepper, and the cayenne pepper. Heat until the butter has melted and the mixture is bubbling around the edges of the pan.

3 Beat in the flour using a wooden spoon, stopping as soon as the mixture is smooth and comes away from the sides of the pan. Remove from the heat and vigorously beat in the eggs and cheeses, until the mixture is smooth, thick and shiny.

4 Spoon into the piping bag and pipe mounds about the size of a walnut onto the lined baking sheets. Dampen your finger with water, lightly press down the tip of each dollop and sprinkle them with Parmesan.

5 Transfer to the heated oven and bake for 8–10 minutes, then reduce the oven temperature to 180°C/350°F/gas 4 and cook for a further 12–15 minutes or until golden brown, puffed and crisp.

THINKING AHEAD

To make the gougères ahead of time, make the mixture and leave in its piping bag in a cool place (but not in the fridge) for up to 3 hours. Alternatively, you can freeze the cooked, cooled gougères and defrost them before warming through for 5 minutes in a hot oven. Though they will still be delicious, these won't be quite as melt-in-the-mouth-light as they are when freshly made.

HAGGIS SCOTCH EGGS

Party food at its finest, the Scotch egg is a thing of beauty, especially in this mini, quail-egg version. The haggis adds a subtle hint to the filling and will convert the minds of those who think they aren't haggis fans.

MAKES 12

12 quail eggs, at room temperature
300g sausagemeat
200g haggis, crumbled
a small bunch of fresh flat-leaf parsley, finely chopped
50g plain flour, seasoned

2 medium eggs, beaten
100g fresh breadcrumbs
vegetable oil, for deep-frying
salt and black pepper

For the aïoli
2 medium egg yolks
2 garlic cloves, crushed

2 teaspoons white wine vinegar
150–200ml groundnut oil
50ml olive oil
a squeeze of lemon juice

1 Bring a pan of water to the boil, add the quail eggs and cook for 1½ minutes. Remove with a slotted spoon and plunge into a bowl of iced water. Once cold, peel away the shells, taking care as the eggs will be very soft.

2 Mix the sausagemeat with the haggis and parsley and season with salt and pepper. Fry a small amount to taste, and adjust the seasoning accordingly. Take about 40g of the mixture, flatten into a disc and gently wrap it evenly around a peeled quail egg to fully enclose, taking care not to squash the egg. Repeat with the remaining meat and eggs. Place on a lined baking sheet and chill in the fridge while you make the aïoli.

3 Whisk the egg yolks with the garlic, vinegar and some salt and pepper. Whisking constantly, gradually pour in the groundnut oil in a very thin, steady stream. Once it is incorporated, add the olive oil in the same way. You should have a glossy, thick sauce. Add the squeeze of lemon juice and check the seasoning.

4 Put the seasoned flour, beaten eggs and breadcrumbs into 3 separate bowls. Dust the Scotch eggs in the flour, then dip in the egg to coat and finally roll in the breadcrumbs.

5 Heat the oil for deep-frying in a large, heavy-bottomed pan or deep-fat fryer to 170°C or until a small piece of bread browns in 30 seconds. Using a slotted spoon, lower the Scotch eggs into the hot oil in batches of 3 or 4 at a time. Fry for 4–5 minutes until golden and cooked, then remove with a slotted spoon to drain on a kitchen tray lined with kitchen paper. Repeat with the remaining eggs and serve with the aïoli to dip them in.

TIP

When making mayonnaise, you need to add the oil in a very thin, steady stream and whisk constantly to emulsify it in the yolks; it helps to have another person to pour whilst you whisk. If the mayonnaise starts to look greasy it may be in danger of splitting. Try adding a little splash of ice-cold water or, if it is really on the edge, add another egg yolk and whisk like mad until it comes back together.

RED ONION, PANCETTA AND SAGE PUFF TART

This is an unusual but great way of using puff pastry as a tart case. The preheated baking sheet ensures that the bottom of the tart gets lots of heat and cooks properly.

SERVES 8
YOU WILL NEED: A 30 X 20CM SWISS ROLL TIN

375g sheet of ready-rolled
    all-butter puff pastry, thawed
    if frozen
2 tablespoons olive oil
a knob of unsalted butter
2 red onions, finely sliced
7–8 fresh sage leaves, finely
    sliced

300g baby spinach
250ml crème fraîche
3 large eggs
65g Gruyère cheese, grated
95g pancetta rashers, torn
    lengthways
salt and black pepper

1 Unroll the pastry and use to line the base and sides of the swiss roll tin. Prick the base all over with a fork and chill. Meanwhile, heat the oven to 200°C/400°F/gas 6 and put a baking sheet in to heat up.

2 Heat the oil and butter in a frying pan over a low heat and cook the onion and sage for 15 minutes until lovely and soft. Transfer to a bowl, then add the spinach to the pan and cook, stirring, until wilted. Remove from the pan and refresh under cold running water before squeezing out as much water as possible. Roughly chop and add to the onion.

3 Beat together the crème fraîche, eggs and most of the cheese, and season well. Spread the spinach mixture over the pastry, then pour over the creamy egg mixture and top with the pancetta and remaining cheese. Transfer to the hot baking sheet in the heated oven and bake for 25–30 minutes until the pastry is puffed and the filling set and golden.

TARTIFLETTE

The classic skier's dish that you normally wouldn't be advised to eat in large amounts unless you have been on the slopes all day in minus degrees. It tastes so good and is so simple to make and serve that it is perfect party food, although you might want to make sure you get involved in an energetic eightsome reel to get you ready! Pictured overleaf.

SERVES 6
YOU WILL NEED: A 1.6 LITRE OVENPROOF DISH

1kg waxy potatoes
1 tablespoon olive oil
a knob of butter
250g smoked bacon lardons
1 large onion, finely sliced
1 garlic clove, finely sliced

100ml dry white wine
200ml double cream
300g Reblochon cheese,
 thickly sliced
salt and black pepper

1 Heat the oven to 190°C/375°F/gas 5. Cook the potatoes (unpeeled) in a pan of boiling salted water for 10-12 minutes, until just tender. Drain and thickly slice.

2 Heat the oil and butter in a frying pan and fry the lardons until starting to crisp. Stir in the onion and fry for a further 5-10 minutes until tender. Add the garlic and wine and bubble until the wine is almost gone. Season, remove from the heat and stir through the cream and potato slices.

3 Layer the potato mixture with most of the cheese slices in an ovenproof dish, pouring over any remaining cream from the pan at the end, before topping with a final layer of cheese. Transfer to the heated oven and bake for 25-30 minutes until golden and bubbling.

PUMPKIN AND COCONUT TARTLETS

For something a little different, these creamy spice-filled tarts make a great starter or substantial nibble at a party. The pine nuts in the pastry make it quite delicate, so be patient, and if it starts to warm up too quickly, pop it back into the fridge for 10 minutes to make it easier to handle.

MAKES 6
YOU WILL NEED: 6 X 10CM LOOSE-BOTTOMED, FLUTED TART TINS

2 tablespoons olive oil

1 large banana shallot, finely chopped

2 garlic cloves, crushed

1 red chilli, finely chopped

200g pumpkin, cut into 1.5cm chunks

75ml vegetable or chicken stock

a good grating of fresh nutmeg

160ml tin coconut cream, chilled

125ml double cream

1 medium egg and 2 yolks

a small bunch of fresh coriander, finely chopped

salt and black pepper

For the pastry

200g plain flour, plus extra for dusting

45g pine nuts

150g cold unsalted butter, diced

1 medium egg yolk

2 tablespoons ice-cold water

1 To make the pastry, whizz the flour and pine nuts together in a food processor until the nuts are finely chopped. Add the butter and pulse until it resembles fine breadcrumbs. Add the egg yolk and enough cold water to just bring it together as you pulse. Alternatively, chop the pine nuts as finely as you can before adding to the flour, rubbing in the butter with your fingertips and mixing in the water using a knife. Once it has all come together, knead briefly until smooth then shape into a disc, wrap in clingfilm and chill for 15 minutes. Meanwhile, heat the oven to 200°C/400°F/gas 6.

2 Roll out the chilled pastry on a lightly floured surface and use to line the tart tins. Line each with baking paper and fill with ceramic baking beans or rice. Place the tins on a baking sheet, transfer to the heated oven and blind bake for 10 minutes until the pastry is set. Remove the paper and beans and return to the oven for a further 3–4 minutes until lightly golden. Reduce the oven temperature to 170°C/325°F/gas 3.

3 Meanwhile, to make the filling, heat the oil in a saucepan and gently fry the shallot for 10 minutes, then add the garlic, chilli and pumpkin. Cook for a couple of minutes, then pour over the stock, cover and cook for 12–15 minutes until the pumpkin is tender. Drain and whizz to a smooth purée. Season well with salt, pepper and nutmeg, and set aside to cool.

4 Scrape off all the thick cream from the top of the chilled tin of coconut (about two-thirds of the tin) and add to the pumpkin with the double cream, egg and yolks, and coriander. Check the seasoning, then pour into the tart cases. Transfer the tins, on the baking sheet, to the heated oven and bake for 20–25 minutes until just set and lightly golden. Cool in the tins for 10 minutes before turning out and serving.

INDULGENT FISH PIE

Fish pie is one of those dishes that always hits the spot. Unlike many, this one doesn't involve cooking the fish first; that way, it doesn't overcook and all its flavour is released into your pie.

〜〜〜〜〜〜〜〜〜〜〜〜〜〜〜〜〜〜

SERVES 6
YOU WILL NEED: A 1.5 LITRE OVENPROOF DISH

1kg floury potatoes, peeled and chopped
225ml double cream
350ml full-fat milk
2 fresh bay leaves
2 sprigs of fresh rosemary
75g butter, plus extra for dotting on the pie
75g plain flour
1 tablespoon Dijon mustard

a small handful of fresh flat-leaf parsley, chopped
100g watercress, chopped
500g sustainable firm, skinless white fish, such as haddock, cod or pollack, cut into chunks
200g sustainable, undyed smoked haddock, skinned and cut into chunks

200g small raw Atlantic prawns, peeled
3 medium eggs, boiled for 7 minutes, peeled and quartered
salt and black pepper

〜〜〜〜〜〜〜〜〜〜〜〜〜〜〜〜〜〜

1 Place the potatoes in a pan of cold, salted water, bring to the boil and simmer for 12–15 minutes until tender. Drain and mash well with 2–3 tablespoons of the double cream and 50ml of the milk. Season and set aside.

2 To make the sauce, heat the rest of the cream and milk with the bay leaves and rosemary until almost boiling, then pour into a large jug and set aside to infuse. Rinse out the pan.

3 Melt the butter in the pan, add the flour and cook for 1–2 minutes. Gradually add the infused milk and cream, discarding the herbs. Stir constantly until you have a smooth thick sauce. Return to the heat, season and bubble for a further minute or two. Don't worry that it is very thick at this point as the fish will add its juices to the sauce as it cooks. Stir in the mustard, parsley and watercress and set aside to cool. Heat the oven to 200°C/400°F/gas 6.

4 Mix the fish and prawns into the cooled sauce and tip into an ovenproof dish. Add the eggs, pushing them into the fish mixture, then spoon over the mashed potato. Rough up the surface using a fork, then dot all over with a little butter.

5 Place in the heated oven and bake for 30–35 minutes or until bubbling underneath and golden brown on top. Divide among plates and serve with buttered peas.

CHOCOLATE, COFFEE AND RUM TORTE

Everyone needs something seriously chocolatey in their culinary repertoire for die-hard chocoholics, and this will definitely hit the spot.

SERVES 10

YOU WILL NEED: A 23CM ROUND SPRINGFORM OR LOOSE-BOTTOMED CAKE TIN, GREASED AND LINED

200g unsalted butter, diced
200g dark chocolate
   (70% cocoa solids),
   broken into pieces
4 large eggs
200g caster sugar

100g ground almonds
50g plain flour
1 tablespoon instant espresso
   powder
3 tablespoons dark rum
cocoa powder, for dusting

1 Heat the oven to 180°C/350°F/gas 4. Melt the butter and chocolate together in a heatproof bowl set over a pan of barely simmering water. Stir until smooth, then set aside to cool slightly.

2 Meanwhile, using a hand-held electric whisk, beat the eggs and sugar until they are really voluminous and pale and the beaters leave a trail in the mixture when lifted out. This will take a good 5–10 minutes.

3 Carefully fold the melted butter and chocolate into the egg mixture, trying not to knock out all the air. Mix the ground almonds, flour and espresso powder together and carefully fold into the egg mixture, then fold in the rum.

Pour into the prepared tin, place in the heated oven and bake for 35–40 minutes until the top is nicely set and a skewer inserted into the centre comes out almost clean.

4 Leave to cool in the tin for 10 minutes then carefully turn out onto a wire rack to cool completely. Dust all over with cocoa powder before serving with vanilla ice cream.

TIP

Frangelico, Baileys, Amaretto or Bourbon would all work brilliantly in place of the rum.

PAUL'S BLACK BUN

SERVES 10–12

YOU WILL NEED: A 900G LOAF TIN, LINED WITH GREASEPROOF PAPER

For the pastry
300g plain flour
75g lard, cubed
75g butter, cubed
a pinch of salt
½ teaspoon baking powder
4 tablespoons cold water
1 small egg, beaten

For the filling
200g plain flour
300g raisins
300g currants
½ teaspoon ground ginger
½ teaspoon ground cinnamon
½ teaspoon ground allspice
½ teaspoon ground mixed
   spice
¼ teaspoon ground black
   pepper
100g dark muscovado sugar
100g mixed peel, chopped
½ teaspoon bicarbonate
   of soda
2 tablespoons whisky
1 medium egg
3 tablespoons buttermilk

1 For the pastry, sift the flour into a bowl and rub in the lard and butter with your fingertips until the mixture resembles breadcrumbs. Add the salt, baking powder and water and mix to a soft dough. Turn out and knead into a ball. Wrap in clingfilm and chill while you make the filling.

2 Heat the oven to 180°C/350°F/gas 4. In a large bowl, mix the flour, raisins, currants, spices, sugar, mixed peel, bicarbonate of soda, whisky, egg and buttermilk together.

3 On a lightly floured surface, roll out two-thirds of the pastry to a rectangle large enough to line the tin. Drape into the tin and press up against the sides. Spoon the filling into the tin, pressing down so it is dense.

4 Roll out three-quarters of the remaining pastry to a rectangle large enough to cover the tin. Dampen the edges of the pastry with water and press the pastry lid on top to seal. Trim the edges and crimp using the tines of a fork. Roll out the remaining pastry with any trimmings and use to make a bow to decorate the top, then attach it to the top with a little water.

5 Brush with the beaten egg, transfer to the heated oven and bake for 2 hours. Remove from the oven and leave to cool in the tin before turning out.

PASSION FRUIT AND POMEGRANATE PAVLOVA LAYER CAKE

A beautifully tiered pavlova will make an impressive centrepiece
for everyone to gather around at a celebration.

SERVES 12–16

10 medium egg whites
525g caster sugar

For the topping and filling
4 passion fruit, scooped out
  and sieved, seeds discarded
3 tablespoons caster sugar

750ml double cream
2 tablespoons Cointreau
3 tablespoons orange curd
3 tablespoons lemon curd
zest of 2 limes, thinly pared
seeds of 2 pomegranates
runny honey, for drizzling

1 Heat the oven to 110°C/225°F/gas ¼. Line 3 baking sheets with baking paper, then draw a 27cm circle on one sheet and a 22cm circle and an 18cm circle on the other sheets.

2 Whisk the egg whites in a large bowl using a hand-held electric whisk, until they form stiff peaks. Still whisking, add the sugar, a little at a time, until the mixture is thick and glossy.

3 Spoon half the mixture over the largest circle, and divide the rest between the smaller two, putting slightly more on the middle-sized circle. Use the back of a spoon to spread the mixture to the edges of your circles and make pretty swirls and peaks. Transfer to the heated oven and cook for 5 hours, then turn off the heat and leave in the oven to cool completely.

4 To assemble, stir the passion fruit juice and sugar into the double cream – the mixture will thicken with the acid from the juice. Stir in the Cointreau and curds to make a luscious thick cream. If it is not thick enough (some passion fruit are juicier than others), whisk a little; if too thick, add a splash more cream.

5 Place the largest meringue on a flat serving plate and spoon over one-third of the cream. Scatter with some pomegranate seeds and lime zest. Top with the second largest meringue and spoon over another third of cream and more seeds and zest. Top with the smallest meringue and finish with the rest of the cream, seeds and zest. Drizzle all over with the honey and serve.

TIP

Keep your egg yolks for custards or quiches. You need to add a pinch of sugar or salt (depending on whether you want them for sweet or savoury dishes) and beat well before freezing in freezer bags or small containers. Label how many yolks you have and whether they are sweet or savoury. Defrost in the fridge before using.

EGGNOG CUSTARD TART

Beloved by Americans over the holiday season, eggnog is a strange drink, which somehow makes so much more sense in a tart. The silky custard is just set with a luscious wobble, while the Bourbon gives the dessert a warming glow.

SERVES 8–10
YOU WILL NEED: A 23CM FLUTED LOOSE-BOTTOMED TART TIN

For the filling
450ml double cream
60ml Bourbon
8 large egg yolks, beaten
1 teaspoon vanilla extract
60g caster sugar
2 teaspoons cornflour

a couple of good gratings
of nutmeg

For the pastry
3 large egg yolks
85g cold unsalted butter,
cut into chunks

85g caster sugar
170g plain flour, plus extra
for dusting
a pinch of salt

1 To make the pastry, whizz the egg yolks and butter in a food processor until light and fluffy (or you could use a hand-held electric whisk). Gradually pulse in the sugar, then the flour and salt, until the pastry comes together. Turn out onto a lightly floured surface and knead the dough together gently and quickly with your hands. Shape into a disc, wrap in clingfilm and chill in the fridge for 1 hour.

2 Roll out the chilled pastry on a lightly floured surface to the thickness of a £1 coin and use to line the tart tin. Chill again in the fridge for 30 minutes, or in the freezer for 15 minutes. Heat the oven to 190°C/375°F/gas 5.

3 Line the pastry case with baking paper and fill completely with ceramic baking beans or rice. Place in the heated oven and blind bake for 20 minutes, then remove the beans and paper. Turn the temperature down to 170°C/325°F/gas 3 and cook for a further 5–10 minutes until the pastry is golden and crisp. Remove from the oven and leave to cool.

4 Turn the temperature down to 130°C/250°F/gas ½. Heat the cream and Bourbon in a pan until almost boiling. Stir the egg yolks, the vanilla extract and sugar in a bowl until well combined, add the cornflour and a good grating of nutmeg, then pour over the hot cream and Bourbon.

5 Strain the mixture through a sieve into a jug, then place the tart on a baking sheet and pour the filling into the tart case. Add another grating of nutmeg, transfer to the warm oven and bake for 35–40 minutes until set but still with a gentle wobble when you move it. Remove from the oven and allow to cool completely before serving.

TIP

The best way to line the tart case is to roll the pastry out to slightly larger than the tin, slip the loose bottom of the tin under the pastry and carefully fold the edges in towards the centre. You can then drop the bottom into the tart case, unfurl the pastry and press it into place.

FRANGELICO AND ROASTED HAZELNUT BAKED CHEESECAKE

A heavenly cheesecake to tempt even the most staunch non-dessert eaters into submission.

SERVES 8–10
YOU WILL NEED: A 22CM ROUND, LOOSE-BOTTOMED
OR SPRINGFORM CAKE TIN, WELL GREASED

For the base
100g digestive biscuits
75g dark chocolate digestive biscuits
50g roasted chopped hazelnuts
20g caster sugar
a good pinch of fine sea salt

85g unsalted butter, melted, plus extra for greasing

For the filling
600g full-fat cream cheese, at room temperature
180g caster sugar
200ml soured cream, at room temperature

3 large eggs, at room temperature
75ml Frangelico
1 teaspoon vanilla extract
60g plain flour, sifted

150ml double cream
125g dark chocolate, broken into chunks

1 To make the base, whizz all the biscuits in a food processor to fine crumbs. Add the hazelnuts, sugar, salt and melted butter and pulse until it resembles wet sand. Alternatively, put the biscuits in a sealed plastic food bag wrapped in a tea towel and crush with a rolling pin, then transfer to a bowl and stir in the other ingredients. Press the mixture evenly into the greased tin, then chill for at least 30 minutes.

2 Heat the oven to 170°C/325°F/gas 3. Mix the cream cheese, sugar and soured cream together in a medium bowl until smooth – don't over beat. Gently beat in the eggs, one at a time, then add the Frangelico and vanilla. Whisk in the flour to form a smooth batter.

3 Remove the tin from the fridge and pour the filling over the base. Put the tin on a baking sheet, place in the heated oven and bake for

50–60 minutes until the top is golden, set at the edges but just wobbly in the middle. Leave to cool completely in the tin. When cool, transfer to the fridge to set for at least 3 hours or overnight.

4 To serve, put the cream in a small pan and heat until almost boiling. Put the chocolate in a bowl, pour over the hot cream and allow to melt, then stir until smooth. Spread over the top of the cheesecake and allow to cool before serving.

TIP

Bringing your filling ingredients to room temperature before beating them together will stop them curdling and also reduce the chance of the mixture splitting to form cracks as it cooks.

MACARONS

These little French fancies can be a little temperamental, as they are affected by temperature and humidity, but a little practice should see you making perfect macarons. A stack of pastel-pale pâtisserie makes an impressive centrepiece for your party. Pictured overleaf.

MAKES 20
YOU WILL NEED: A PIPING BAG, FITTED WITH A 1CM PLAIN NOZZLE

175g icing sugar
125g ground almonds
3 large egg whites
a pinch of salt
75g caster sugar
1 teaspoon vanilla extract

For the filling
150g unsalted butter,
 softened
75g icing sugar
75g chocolate spread or
 flavourings of your choice
 (see Tip)

1 Heat the oven to 170°C/325°F/gas 3 and line 2 baking sheets with non-stick baking paper. Whizz the icing sugar and ground almonds in a food processor to a very fine mixture, then sift into a bowl.

2 Whisk the egg whites and salt to soft peaks in a separate large bowl, then gradually whisk in the caster sugar until thick and glossy. Add the vanilla extract and whisk in. Fold in half the almond and icing sugar mixture, then add the second half using a spatula to cut and fold the mixture until it is shiny and has a thick, ribbon-like consistency (it will take about 30 folds with your spatula). Spoon into a piping bag.

3 Pipe small rounds of the macaron mixture, about 2cm diameter (they will spread once piped), onto the baking sheets, then give the baking sheets a sharp tap on the work surface to ensure a good 'foot'. Leave to stand at room temperature for 10-15 minutes to form a slight skin. This is important – you should be able to touch them lightly without any mixture sticking to your finger.

4 Transfer the baking sheets to the heated oven and bake for 15 minutes. Remove from the oven, slide the macarons on the baking paper onto a wire rack and cool completely before peeling each one carefully off the paper.

5 Meanwhile, to make the filling, beat the butter in a bowl until light and fluffy, then beat in the icing sugar and chocolate spread. Sandwich the cold macarons together with a little of the filling.

TIP

You can make a simple buttercream by omitting the chocolate spread and use citrus zest or other flavourings instead.

For pistachio macarons, replace half the ground almonds with ground pistachios (whizz in a blender with a little of the flour) and use green food colouring to achieve a pastel green. Fold chopped pistachios through a buttercream filling, if you like.

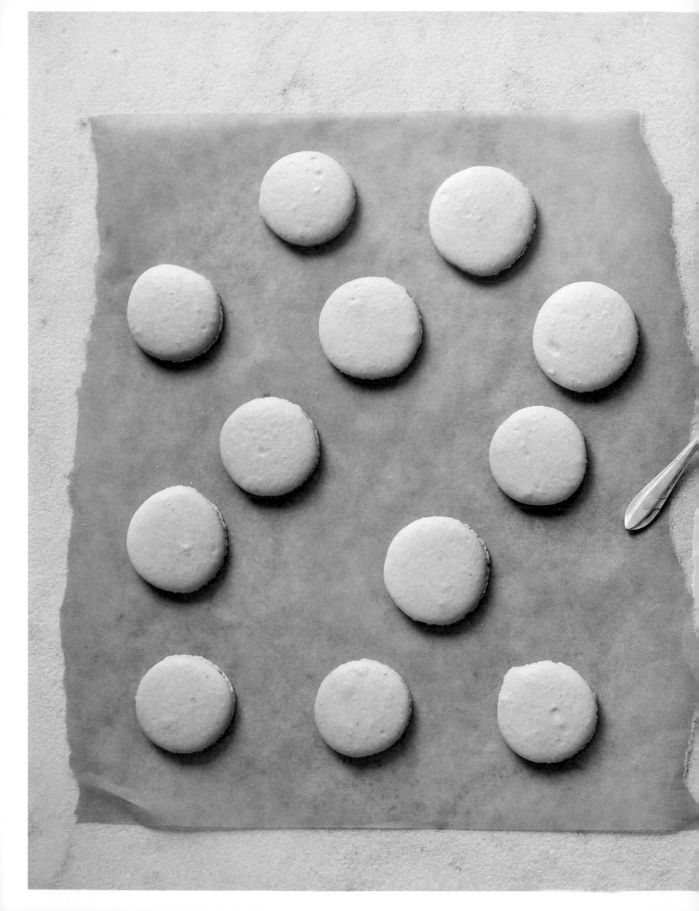

TRIFLE WITH HOMEMADE MADEIRA CAKE

A true British classic, this overly large bowl of beautifully layered boozy trifle is a winner. The homemade Madeira cake is well worth the extra effort. What better way to see in the New Year?

SERVES 8–10

YOU WILL NEED: A 900G LOAF TIN, GREASED AND LINED; A 2.5 LITRE TRIFLE BOWL

125ml Madeira or sweet sherry

450ml double cream

2 tablespoons icing sugar

2 tablespoons brandy

For the poached pears

5 firm, ripe pears, peeled

pared zest of 1 lemon

1 cinnamon stick, snapped
  in half

4 cloves

200g caster sugar

1 bottle full-bodied red wine

For the cake

175g unsalted butter

175g caster sugar

finely grated zest of 1 lemon

½ teaspoon vanilla extract

3 large eggs

200g self-raising flour

50g ground almonds

For the custard

350ml double cream

350ml full-fat milk

1 vanilla pod, slit in half
  lengthways and seeds
  scraped

4 medium egg yolks

2 tablespoons cornflour

75g caster sugar

2 leaves of gelatine

1 Put the pears in a pan with the pared zest, cinnamon, cloves, sugar and wine. Bring to a simmer and cook very gently for 15–20 minutes until tender to the point of a knife. Leave to cool in the liquid.

2 To make the cake, heat the oven to 180°C/ 350°F/gas 4. Whisk the butter with the sugar using a hand-held electric whisk until light and fluffy, then add the lemon zest and vanilla. Gradually beat in the eggs, one at a time, whisking well between each addition. Fold in the flour and ground almonds and spoon into the prepared loaf tin, smoothing the top.

3 Place the cake in the heated oven and bake for 40–50 minutes or until a skewer inserted into the centre comes out clean. Leave to cool in

the tin for 10 minutes then turn out onto a wire rack and leave to cool completely.

4 Meanwhile, to make the custard, put the cream and milk into a heavy-based saucepan and add the vanilla seeds and pod. Whisk together the egg yolks, cornflour and sugar in a bowl. Soak the gelatine in a small bowl of cold water. Bring the cream mixture to a gentle simmer, then pour, with the vanilla pod, onto the egg mixture, whisking constantly to prevent curdling. Return to the cleaned-out pan and stir over a low heat until the mixture thickens – it should thickly coat the back of a spoon – and spoon into a bowl. Squeeze the water from the gelatine, add it to the custard and stir to dissolve. Cover the surface with clingfilm to stop a skin forming. Leave to cool completely.

CONTINUED

5 Once the cake is cold, cut it into 5cm cubes (if you have a little too much for your bowl keep the rest for eating with a cup of tea) and arrange in the bottom of the trifle bowl, then sprinkle with the Madeira or sherry. Slice the poached pears into halves, remove the cores, and arrange on top of the cake in the bowl.

6 Remove the vanilla pod from the cooled custard and dollop the custard all over the fruit, then put in the fridge to firm up fully for an hour or so. When ready to serve, whisk the cream, icing sugar and brandy together until it forms soft peaks. Spoon it over the custard and serve immediately.

THINKING AHEAD

Start your trifle well in advance. You can make the cake and poach the pears the day before, then make the custard and assemble the trifle on the day itself.

ALMOND, HAZELNUT AND WHITE CHOCOLATE LAYER CAKE

This cake really is a showstopper, with six layers of delicate sponge coated in a white chocolate mousse icing. It looks beautiful unadorned but if you want to decorate it to more impressive heights, make some chocolate holly leaves and add coated sugared almonds. Pictured overleaf.

SERVES 12–14
YOU WILL NEED: 3 X 18CM ROUND, LOOSE-BOTTOMED
SANDWICH TINS, BUTTERED AND LINED

For the icing
3 leaves of gelatine
700ml double cream
300g white chocolate, broken
   into pieces
4 tablespoons Frangelico

For the hazelnut sponge
275g unsalted butter, softened
275g caster sugar

5 medium eggs
50g roasted chopped
   hazelnuts
250g self-raising flour
50g ground almonds

To decorate (optional)
white chocolate holly leaves
   (see Tip)
sugar coated almonds

1 For the icing, soak the gelatine in a bowl of cold water for a couple of minutes. Meanwhile, put 350ml of the cream into a pan. Bring to the boil, then remove from the heat. Remove the gelatine from the water and squeeze out as much excess water as possible. Add to the cream, stirring until dissolved.

2 Put the white chocolate in a food processor and, with the motor running, slowly add the hot cream in a steady stream. Whizz until smooth, then spoon into a bowl, cover with clingfilm and leave to cool. Chill for about 30 minutes.

3 Whisk the remaining cream with the Frangelico to stiff peaks, then fold into the chilled chocolate

mixture. Cover with clingfilm and chill for up to 3 hours.

4 Heat the oven to 180°C/350°F/gas 4. Beat the butter and sugar together using a hand-held electric whisk until light and fluffy. Add the eggs, one at a time, beating really well before adding the next.

5 Whizz the hazelnuts in a food processor with 100g of the flour. Fold this and the rest of the flour and the ground almonds into the sponge mixture. Divide between the prepared tins, place in the heated oven and bake for 30 minutes until the sponges are golden and a skewer inserted into the centre comes out clean.

CONTINUED

6 Turn out the sponges onto a wire rack and leave to cool. Once cool, slice each in half horizontally to make six layers. Put one sponge base on a serving plate or cake stand. Using a palette knife, spread a layer of the icing, then repeat with the remaining sponge layers. Cover the sides and top of the cake with the icing (working quickly as the icing will soften as you work; if it becomes too soft, chill the icing and the cake for 30 minutes). Decorate with chocolate holly leaves (see Tip) and sugared almonds, if you like.

TIP

To make chocolate holly leaves, melt 50g white chocolate in a bowl over a pan of barely simmering water, making sure the base of the bowl is not touching the water. Wash and dry some fresh holly leaves, brush them all over on the underside of the leaf with the melted chocolate and leave to set. Carefully peel the leaf away from the chocolate, and add the chocolate leaves to the top of the cake.

FRANCES' SUGAR AND SPICE STELLAR CUPCAKES

Christmas is all about surprises – and mincemeat! – so I've incorporated both in these cupcakes with a hidden mincemeat centre. Brandy buttercream works as the perfect accompaniment to the marzipan stars on top, but you could also use Amaretto, or omit the alcohol altogether – they'll still be packed with Christmas sparkle!

THE GREAT
BRITISH BAKE OFF
**FRANCES
QUINN**
2013

MAKES 12
**YOU WILL NEED: A 12-HOLE CUPCAKE OR MUFFIN TIN, LINED
WITH CUPCAKE CASES; 1 SMALL AND 1 MINI STAR CUTTER**

For the cupcakes
150g slightly salted butter,
  softened
150g caster sugar
3 medium eggs, beaten
1 teaspoon almond extract
150g self-raising flour
3 tablespoons ground almonds
1 teaspoon ground mixed spice

**For the marzipan stars,
filling and decoration**
150g white marzipan
icing sugar, for dusting
silver balls
250g mincemeat
gold and silver edible glitter

For the brandy buttercream
100g slightly salted butter,
  softened
200g icing sugar
1 teaspoon vanilla extract
1 tablespoon brandy

1 Heat the oven to 180°C/350°F/gas 4.

2 Beat the butter and sugar together in a bowl to a lightly creamy consistency. Gradually beat in the eggs, one-third at a time, followed by the almond extract. Sift in the flour and fold in with the ground almonds and mixed spice, until combined.

3 Divide the mixture between the cases, transfer to the heated oven and bake for 10–15 minutes, until risen and lightly golden brown and a skewer inserted into the centre of one comes out clean. Set aside to cool slightly before removing the cupcakes to a wire rack to cool completely.

4 Meanwhile, to make the marzipan stars, roll out the marzipan to about a 3mm thickness on a surface lightly dusted with icing sugar. Using the cutters, stamp out 12 small stars and 36 mini stars, re-rolling the trimmings as you go. Lay them out on a tray and carefully press a cluster of 3 silver balls into the small stars and 1 into the centre of the mini ones. Leave to dry out completely.

5 Once the cupcakes have cooled, use a small knife or 3–4cm cookie cutter to scoop out the centre of each cupcake. Spoon mincemeat into the cavity of each and replace the cake tops.

6 To make the brandy buttercream, beat the butter, icing sugar, vanilla and brandy in a bowl for several minutes until smooth, light and very pale. Transfer the mixture to a disposable piping bag and snip off 2.5cm from the end. Pipe the buttercream on top of each cupcake and decorate with the marzipan stars. Sprinkle over a very light dusting of edible glitter.

JO'S CHOCOLATE FRUIT AND NUT BUBBLE WRAP CAKE

THE GREAT
BRITISH BAKE OFF
JO
WHEATLEY
2011

For me the excitement of Christmas and New Year starts mid-October. I love to bake ahead, then pop my bakes into the freezer to give me much needed time and energy nearer to the festivities. This is a perfect cake for the festive period, and a great alternative for those who don't like traditional fruit cake. The bubbly chocolate around the sides gives real wow factor to any tea table.

SERVES 18–20

YOU WILL NEED: 2 X 20CM ROUND, SPRINGFORM CAKE TINS, BUTTERED AND BASE-LINED WITH BUTTERED BAKING PAPER; A LENGTH OF CLEAN PLASTIC BUBBLE WRAP; A GOLD RIBBON

175g unsalted butter, softened

300g caster sugar

3 large eggs, beaten

125g self-raising flour

150g plain flour

1 teaspoon bicarbonate of soda

75g cocoa powder

200ml soured cream, at room temperature

50g full-fat cream cheese, at room temperature

100g raisins

100g hazelnuts

For the ganache
300ml double cream

250g dark chocolate, chopped

150g milk chocolate, chopped

For the decorative bubble wrap, and to finish

250g milk chocolate

1 white chocolate bar

gold edible shimmer spray

1 Heat the oven to 180°C/350°F/gas 4. Beat the butter and sugar together using an electric mixer until pale, light and fluffy. Gradually add the beaten eggs, a little at a time, beating well between each addition.

2 Sift the flours, the bicarbonate of soda and cocoa powder into a bowl. Add half of the sifted dry ingredients to the creamed mixture and fold in using a large metal spoon.

3 Mix the soured cream and cream cheese together in another bowl until smooth. Add half to the cake batter and fold in. Fold in the remaining dry ingredients, then the remaining soured cream mixture, and mix until smooth.

4 Stir in two-thirds of the raisins and hazelnuts and spoon the mixture into the prepared tins. Push the remaining raisins and nuts just beneath the surface and level the top with a palette knife.

5 Place on the middle shelf of the heated oven and bake for about 35 minutes or until a skewer inserted into the centre of one cake comes out clean, covering them loosely with foil about halfway through if they are browning too much. Leave to cool in the tin for 10 minutes before turning out onto a wire rack to cool completely.

6 Meanwhile, to make the ganache, bring the cream to the boil in a saucepan. Remove from the heat, add the chopped chocolates and stir

CONTINUED

until smooth and shiny. Cover the surface with clingfilm and allow to cool completely at room temperature.

7 Sandwich the 2 completely cooled cakes together with some of the ganache and transfer to a cake board or serving plate, then cover the top and the sides with two-thirds of the remaining ganache. Chill in the fridge for at least 1 hour, to set. Cover the surface of the remaining ganache with clingfilm and set aside, at room temperature.

8 Meanwhile, to make the decorative bubble wrap, chill 2 baking sheets and melt the milk chocolate in a heatproof bowl set over a pan of simmering water. Cut the plastic bubble wrap into a piece 1cm longer than the circumference of the cake, and a little taller than the depth of the cake, about 10cm. Spread out over the chilled baking sheets placed side by side, pour over the melted milk chocolate and smooth over with a palette knife, ensuring you have a straight edge along the bottom of the bubble wrap that will sit flush with the cake. Leave until almost set, so that the chocolate is dry but still flexible, then wrap around the chilled cake.

9 Beat the remaining ganache to soften it a little, then, leaving the bubble wrap in place, spoon it on top of the cake and spread it to the bubble wrap edges using a small palette knife or spoon. Put back into the fridge to set.

10 Meanwhile, to make chocolate curls, use a swivel peeler to shave ribbons from the narrow side of the white chocolate bar – they will curl up beautifully. Fill the top of the cake with chocolate curls, peel off the plastic bubble wrap, spray with edible gold spray, tie the ribbon around the middle, and enjoy.

TIP

If your kitchen is warm, the ganache might run a little on the sides of the cake. If this happens, place the cake on a wire rack and collect the excess on some greaseproof paper underneath.

THINKING AHEAD

You can freeze the cakes, before the ganache and decorations are added, up to 3 months in advance.

TEMPLATES

TEMPLATES

MARY'S GINGERBREAD HOUSE See page 56

x2

Roof

x2

Front and back
of house

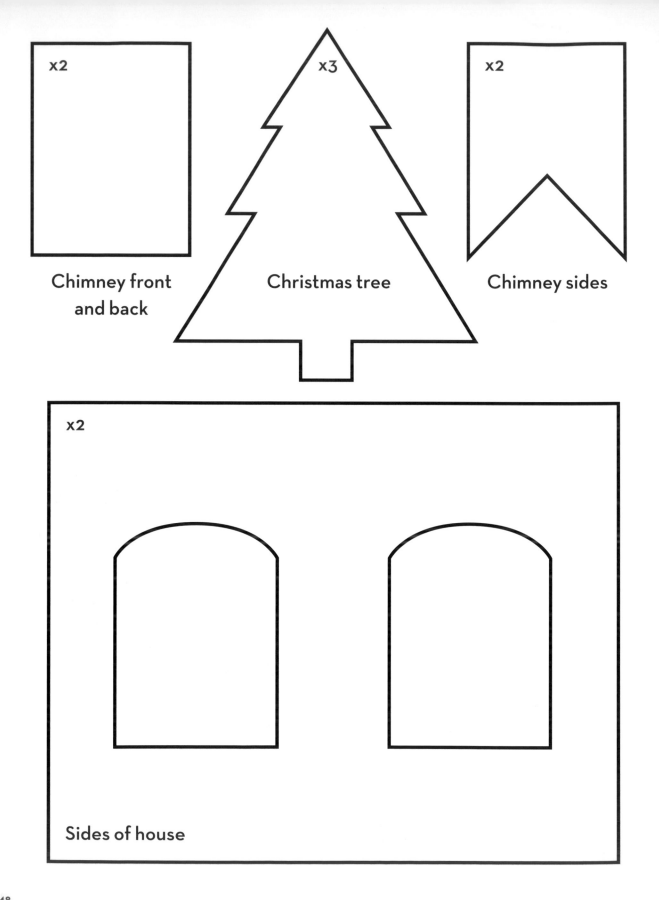

x2

Chimney front
and back

x3

Christmas tree

x2

Chimney sides

x2

Sides of house

PAUL'S ST LUCIA BUNS See page 71

Christmas Cross

S-Shape

Christmas Ox

INDEX

ACKNOWLEDGEMENTS

As a true Christmas obsessive when I was asked to write a beautiful Christmas baking book I jumped at the chance to put my years of festive fanaticism to good use and to share my deep and unshakeable love of all things Christmas (no matter how many times a year it comes) with you all.

This book has been a joy to write and style but I couldn't have done it without my super team, who have made this book what it is.

Ted, your pictures are true works of art and I love them all. Thank you so much for your willingness to shoot well into the night, uproot to Kent for weeks at a time and being generally awesome and full of Christmas spirit and snowballs.

Polly, as ever you are amazing. Without your Polly props, the magical Christmas Drawer, cupboards of well-organised miniature reindeer and your skills as a snow technician this book would never have looked so wonderful. Most importantly, thank you so much for lending us your home to turn into a winter wonderland.

Poppy, my assistant extraordinaire, ever calm and composed and brilliant no matter what. I'd have been lost in a sea of cinnamon and icing sugar without you!

Thank you to all the wonderful bakers who intrepidly trekked to Kent for a fabulous day's shoot in the baking sun and for not minding too much as we tried to force Christmas jumpers over your heads. And a huge thank you, as ever, to my parents for kindly letting us all invade the house! Also to the lovely Bronte at the Scandinavian Kitchen for lending me her kransekake pans to create an epic 18-tiered celebration cake.

Finally, thank you so much to Kate and Lizzy from BBC Books for all their belief, support, understanding and encouragement. I think we have made a real Christmas cracker.

ALSO AVAILABLE FROM

THE GREAT BRITISH BAKE OFF®

How to achieve baking perfection at home, with foolproof recipes and simple step-by-step masterclasses based on Mary and Paul's Technical Challenges.

Baking doesn't have to be complicated to be 'showstopping'. Inspired by the Showstopper Challenge, here are bakes that will both turn heads and make mouths water.

Simple, reliable, delicious bakes for every day — these are the recipes you will return to over and over again.

Packed with practical advice to help you improve your baking. It includes fascinating trivia covering the history of baking and the chemistry crucial to achieving winning bakes.

NEW BOOK

Learn to Bake tells you everything you need to know to bake for every occasion and every person in your life — 80 easy recipes for all the family.

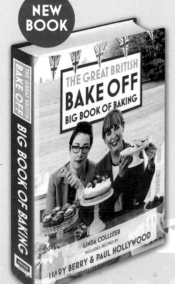

The ultimate guide to baking, whether you are a complete novice or a well-practiced home cook, this book provides you with 120 brand-new recipes that are suitable for every occasion and level of skill.